AR

2

WITHDRAWN

PRIVATE
IRELAND

Publisher *Beatrice Vincenzini*

Executive Director *David Shannon*

Editorial Director *Alexandra Black*

Art Director *David Mackintosh*

Publishing Assistant *Charlotte Wilton-Steer*

Locations Coordinator *Victoria Lloyd*

————

First published in the UK by Scriptum Editions

Created by Co & Bear Productions (UK) Ltd.

Copyright © 1999 Co & Bear Productions(UK) Ltd.

Photographs copyright © 1999 Simon McBride.

Printed and bound in Novara, Italy by
Officine Grafiche de Agostini.

First edition

10 9 8 7 6 5 4 3 2 1

ISBN 1-902686-03-9

PRIVATE
IRELAND

Photographed by SIMON McBRIDE
Written by KAREN HOWES

Introduction by MARIANNE FAITHFULL

SCRIPTUM EDITIONS
LONDON · HONG KONG

CONTENTS

*I*NTRODUCTION *by Marianne Faithfull*

Everyone comes to live in Ireland for different reasons, as many of the people in this evocative study of the country reveal. Some are here because their families have been here for centuries and couldn't imagine living anywhere else. Some are attracted by the landscape; some by the slow pace of life in Irish country villages. Some come to escape, to start out fresh in an environment they see as healing and inspiring, or simply to downsize, to lead a less pressured existence and enjoy life's simple pleasures. Yet others, like me, are lured by the people, by a spirit of community that is rare these days.

I never set out intentionally to move to Ireland; it just seemed to happen that way, perhaps the logical extension of a long-term love affair with the place. I first came in 1964 on a tour around Ireland with the Hollies and Freddy and the Dreamers. Two years later I came back with Mick Jagger and Christopher Gibbs to stay with Desmond Guinness – that's when I really started to make friends, and that Ireland really began to make an impression on me. It was great fun in those days. We would drive into Dublin for parties or musical evenings, poetry recitals or some other event held in one of the city's beautiful Georgian houses, and I began to get a feel for life in Ireland. So it is not surprising that when I eventually decided to move to Dublin I wanted to live in an old Georgian house.

In the 1970s I often visited Ireland on tour, but by the early 1980s I had ended up in America, where 'Broken English' became a massive underground hit, and I didn't return for quite a few years. Then, in 1985, my mother in England became ill and I really had to come back to Europe, but I didn't want to live in the UK. I nearly went to Paris, but in the end I came to Ireland because I had friends here. Marina Guinness, whom I had known when she was a child, invited me to stay at her stud farm in Kildare. It was she who convinced me to take Shell Cottage, an eighteenth-century folly on the Carton estate. It was my first home in Ireland and it was a wonderful place in which to live and write.

Eventually I decided that it was time to move to Dublin. At the time I was on the road with the Weimar Cabaret and my friends agreed to help me look. They found an apartment in a Georgian house, and the first time I saw it I knew straightaway that I wanted it. It had the original plasterwork and beautiful proportions but it needed a lot of work. It looked, as I described it then, like a Detroit motel. Over the past few years it has slowly been transformed.

My home in Ireland is different from anywhere else. In London I'm always very busy, working and socialising, but here I live the quiet life. It's my retreat. At weekends I might go to visit friends around Ireland, but most of the time I just rest. And people understand that too – there's no pressure to have to do anything. Dublin is also a very beautiful place to live, and as it's a little slower than London or Paris or New York, it is very appealing. In the end, though, it is the people here that are the real attraction.

ABOVE *Since moving into her apartment, on the top floors of a Georgian house in Dublin, Marianne Faithfull has transformed it into a graceful retreat. Despite Marianne's rebel image, her home is decorated with tasteful furnishings and objects that recall the elegance of the early nineteenth century.*

CHAPTER ONE

GRAND CHARACTER

BENVARDEN • GLENARM CASTLE • GREY ABBEY • CLEGGAN • TULLANISK

IRISH HERITAGE

THE HISTORY OF AN ESTATE IS OFTEN AS UNEXPECTED AS IT IS FASCINATING, AT TIMES WELL DOCUMENTED, AND AT OTHERS RELIANT ON DIARIES AND PERSONAL ACCOUNTS TO PAINT A FULLER PICTURE. Benvarden, not far from the north coast of Co. Antrim, has seen its fortunes fluctuate over the centuries, reflecting changes in ownership as much as government intervention. Precious books of ancient maps reveal how extensive the lands around the house once were, and private correspondence contains descriptions of huge parties given in honour of visiting dignitaries, including a stay of several days' duration by the Duke and Duchess of Northumberland. Their visit is described in a diary extract by then-resident Jane Montgomery in 1827: 'The House was lighted up as bright as oil wax and blazing fires of Bogswood and Turf could make it'.

ABOVE *A detail of the marble fireplace in the former ballroom, which was destroyed by fire in 1940. The interior was reconstructed years later, and is now used as a drawing room.* OPPOSITE *A pair of Regency tapestry chairs stand on either side of a marble fireplace in the small library. On the wall is a tapestry depicting the Siege of 'Derry in 1688 when James II was beaten by the Protestants.*

Originally the seat of the Macnaghten family, Benvarden had not always been so grand. Its name is inextricably linked with that of John Macnaghten who has gone down in the annals of local history as 'Half-Hanged Macnaghten'. To this day there is someone eager to recount the tale of the man who in 1760 shot Mary Anne Knox of Prehen while trying to abduct her. He was sentenced to be hanged but the rope broke during the execution. While an excited crowd urged him to escape, he climbed the scaffold a second time, preferring death to being known for ever after as 'Half-Hanged'.

Heavily in debt, Macnaghten's estates were seized by the government, until his daughter, Cassandra, came of age and fought to have them reinstated. Ironically, though, she married an Englishman and never set foot on Benvarden, which, together with its 5,000 acres of land, was put up for sale. It was bought in 1798 by Hugh Montgomery, opening a new chapter in the history of Benvarden.

Hugh Montgomery had disappeared to America in 1780, and returned having made a fortune. The co-founder of the Montgomery Bank, he enlarged the original modest eighteenth-century house on the estate in 1805 with the addition of two wings with bow-fronted windows for a dining room, drawing room and ballroom. An elegant, cantilevered staircase was erected in the hall. No expense was spared to raise the tone of the property to suit Hugh Montgomery's newly established position in society.

By the time he died in 1822, the bank had expanded and his son, and eventually his grandson, took over the position of chairman. Following in his footsteps, they continued to fill the house with furniture and paintings and to acquire more land until, by 1850, Benvarden boasted over 10,000 acres.

Today, Benvarden is home to another Hugh Montgomery, but the estate has been reduced to a very modest affair – largely as a result of land reclamation laws instituted in 1904. The appearance of the property has also changed since his ancestor's flurry of building work at the turn of the nineteenth century. A fire in 1940 gutted the ballroom and bedrooms above, and when the wing was eventually rebuilt Hugh's parents replaced the original two-room structure with one sixty-foot space. The ivy and creepers, which had once covered the facade and required two gardeners to clip them back all summer long, were also destroyed and the new exterior simply painted thereafter.

Benvarden has always been renowned for its Victorian gardens and over the years these have been much improved with a fruit and vegetable garden and a nursery selling trees and shrubs. The gardens are open to the public for three months every summer, offering a taste of the grandeur that had once so captivated Jane Montgomery.

ABOVE *A George IV Gothic gilt-framed mirror hangs above the fireplace; beside it is one of several mahogany peat buckets made from the ballast brought back in ships from America.*
OPPOSITE *In 1956 Hugh Montgomery's father declared that the dining room should be repapered – in a deep red flocked wallpaper. The Chippendale dining table is laid with a Worcester Chamberlain dinner service.*

RIGHT & BELOW *A Victorian iron bridge spans the mist-shrouded River Bush at the end of the long stretch of frosted lawn which descends from the house.* OPPOSITE *Benvarden was originally a two-storey eighteenth-century house with a central curved bow in each of its two fronts. This view up the gravel drive reveals subsequent additions.*

LEFT *The elegant, semi-circular, cantilevered staircase and oval lightwell on the first floor landing are later additions to the original house, and would likely have been added at the same time as the ballroom in 1800.*
OPPOSITE *The long hallway, on to which all the ground floor reception rooms open, runs the width of the house. Painted a warm shade of salmon pink, it is suffused in morning light.*

18

PALLADIAN MANOR

ABOVE An antique wooden box bears an ornate letter 'A' and the coronet of the Earls of Antrim. OPPOSITE In the hall, the columns and marbling on the walls were installed during the 1930s by then-owner, Angela, Countess of Antrim, a professional sculptor. The sunlit library adjoins the hall.

THE ESTATE ROAD WHICH DESCENDS INTO THE GLEN IS A SHEET OF BLACK ICE AND THE MEADOWS EXTENDING AWAY FROM GLENARM CASTLE ARE WHITE WITH HOAR FROST WHICH SPARKLES IN THE BRIGHT SUNLIGHT. Beyond the turrets and the village is the sea, the North Channel, dividing Ireland and Scotland. It was across this channel that raiding Scots came in 1642 and burned down the original Glenarm, built in 1636 by Randle McDonnel, later first Earl of Antrim, as a hunting lodge and secondary residence. What remained of Glenarm after the raid was still used by the first earl as a place to stay during the hunting season, but it was not until 1750 that it became a permanent residence for the fifth Earl of Antrim and his family.

The castle was rebuilt by Christopher Myers, an English engineer, who transformed the charred ruins into a Palladian mansion with curved colonnades on either side ending in pavilions. The seaward facing facade was given the 'Gothick' embellishment of a turreted and crenellated pediment. Further changes were made in the 1820s when Anne Katherine McDonnell, Countess of Antrim, commissioned plans to be drawn up for a 'fashionably romantic country seat', finally executed in the 1850s.

Like many estates which boast a long and colourful history, Glenarm has had its fair share of fires. In 1929, the resident housekeeper kept an ancient featherless parrot and to keep him warm was inclined to stoke up the fire in her bedroom before going on her rounds. A stray spark caused the top floor to catch fire, allowing enough time for the family portraits and Irish furniture to be carried out onto the lawn. By the time the last piece had been salvaged, the house had all but disappeared. Yet, its rebuilding was unimaginative and any surviving Gothic features were removed. Another fire in 1965

destroyed the vast servants' wing, built in the 1830s, and the remains were pulled down. Only the old kitchen survived – the only room to have been used continuously since the seventeenth century. By the 1960s the estate was falling into decline, its original 330,000 acres in the eighteenth century reduced to the 1,300 acres of the home farm.

Responsibility for Glenarm today rests on the shoulders of Randal Dunluce who remembers the stylish way of life his grandfather continued to lead even when there was no money left to support it. The estate was given to Randal on his twenty-fifth birthday by his father, the fourteenth Earl of Antrim, one of the few earls in the family to earn his living, working as Keeper of Conservation at the Tate Gallery in London for thirty years. Under Randal's guidance, the property has gradually emerged from a deep sleep, shaking off the last decades of decline, modernising and revitalising itself in a new bid for survival. The walled garden has been completely restored, and 100 yards of greenhouses resurrected. The eccentric collection of turrets has been reroofed, and the long neglected estate buildings have been repaired and repainted.

Randal's ambition is to restore Glenarm to a working estate and he has recently reintroduced a shoot, employed a gamekeeper, and is in the process of refurbishing many of the rooms in the castle for shooting guests. Future plans involve decorating, and in some cases modernising, the main reception rooms, which might be used for concerts and conferences. It would have been only too easy for Randal to transform the frosted meadows into a marvellous golf course with a restaurant and club house. The route he has chosen to take needs time and considerable investment, restoring the property by slow degrees, rekindling the magic he remembers as a child.

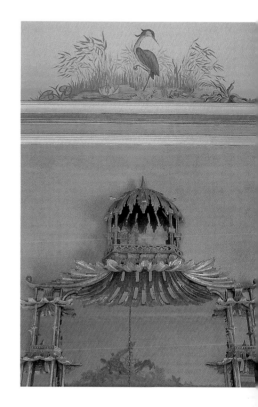

ABOVE *Above the eighteenth-century fireplace at one end of the drawing room hangs a mirror in a gilded chinoiserie frame.* OPPOSITE *The coved ceiling of the formal drawing room was painted in the 1930s with scenes from La Fontaine's fables by Angela, Countess of Antrim. The Empire furniture belonged to her brother, Daniel Sykes.*

OPPOSITE *Among the family portraits in the dining room is a collection of seascapes commissioned by Admiral Lord Mark Kerr, who married into the McDonnell family, which together with the later frieze by Angela, Countess of Antrim, gives the room a distinctly nautical theme.* BELOW *Following the fire in 1929 which destroyed the original interior, Angela decided to redo the hall in a unique style, and began sculpting the gods of the nine planets to act as new caryatids.*

LEFT *An Irish eighteenth-century lion-masked sideboard in the hall is flanked by an Irish nineteenth-century Gothic clock and barometer, specially commissioned for the castle. Above hangs a full-length portrait of Anne Katherine McDonnell.* BELOW *One of a set of late eighteenth-century hall chairs decorated with the family coat of arms.*

ABOVE *Reflected in the curve of a mirror, the Blue Room at Glenarm Castle in Co. Antrim.* RIGHT *Originally the billiard room, the Blue Room today is one of several drawing rooms to benefit from the morning light. It is dominated by paintings of Lord Antrim's racehorses by Thomas Butler – Regulus, White Nose and Starling among them. The paintings date from the mid eighteenth century.*

RIGHT *The Octagon Bedroom, located in one of the turrets at the top of the castle, is the only room which was left untouched during the post-fire rebuilding.* OPPOSITE *The original plaster-work ceiling with doves dates from the late eighteenth century.*

HALLOWED HALL

THE WATERS OF STRANGFORD LOUGH LOOK GREY AND UNINVITING, A STEADY DRIZZLE MISTING THE VIEW OF THE MOURNE MOUNTAINS. From its vantage point above the lough, the facade of Grey Abbey, built of local stone and dulled by today's rain, has taken on the patina of its wintry surroundings. Seat of the Montgomery family since the early sixteenth century, the house is the third to have been built on the site. Little is known of the first house to grace the park of the original Cistercian abbey, but an ancient round stone is considered to be all that remains. The second house accidentally caught fire in 1758, and the present property was started almost immediately in 1760 in the Palladian style so fashionable at the time.

The house as it stands today is not quite true to its original design. When, in 1782, William Montgomery married the Honourable Emilia Ward, the daughter of the first Viscount Bangor, he decided to alter Grey Abbey in the manner of his wife's country seat, Castle Ward, which was famous for having one classical facade and the other Gothic. William added an octagonal, Gothic-inspired drawing room to the garden facade of Grey Abbey, and is also thought to have moved the staircase from the centre of the house to its present location at one end of the property so that the front door did not spoil either facade. An eighteenth-century watercolour shows the carriage drive approaching Grey Abbey through a pair of magnificent Gothic gates, which still exist, sweeping past the ruins of the old abbey and up to the garden side of the house with its Gothic flourishes.

In 1840, another powerful lady married into the Montgomery family. Lady Charlotte Herbert of Powis, a great-granddaughter of Clive of India, raised the roof to add an extra storey to the house, tying it all together with a balustrade around the facade

ABOVE *The sculpted bust of one of many Montgomerys to have lived at Grey Abbey.*
OPPOSITE *A glimpse of the cosy library bathed in evening light. It is furnished with an emphasis on comfort, the armchairs and sofa well-used, and the tables covered in family clutter.*

which cleverly conceals the windows of the upper floor. Fifty years later, the only addition to mar the classical shape of Grey Abbey was the kitchen. It was devised by Victoria Alberta Ponsonby, a member of Souls – a group of intellectual ladies of the day – and another influential woman to marry into the Montgomery dynasty. She is remembered among other things for running compulsory education classes for staff, with the result that most of them could recite Shakespeare's soliloquies word perfectly.

Bill Montgomery and his wife Daphne have been at Grey Abbey for the last thirty years. Bill's position as Sotheby's representative in Northern Ireland, his interest in historic houses and opera, as well as Daphne's reputation for being an excellent hostess, have ensured that the house is used to full advantage. It is difficult to heat in winter, so, when not entertaining, they tend to adopt a lifestyle reminiscent of the eighteenth century, when the Honourable Emilia would choose where to dine, and a table would be laid in the library or the Blue Drawing Room to suit. All that has changed in the intervening years is that Bill and Daphne do not enjoy the services of a footman. Following in the wake of the influential wives who preceded her, Daphne has been developing the gardens. The ha-ha has been revealed, a Victorian orchard of Irish apple trees uncovered, and the seventeenth-century park has been replanted with specimen trees.

Grey Abbey now combines the roles of family home for the Montgomery family, office for Bill and a suitably impressive venue for entertaining Sotheby's clients. It is a delightfully elegant house where business colleagues and friends alike can enjoy lunch or dinner, followed by a quick tour of the restored gardens, where Daphne is happy to point out the regenerated orchard that now bears ancient strains of Irish apple.

ABOVE *A fine collection of late eighteenth- and early nineteenth-century glass graces a shelf in the middle drawing room.*
OPPOSITE *The octagonal Gothic dining room was formerly a rarely used drawing room added to the property at the end of the eighteenth century. Daphne had always been convinced that the imaginative shape would make it a more interesting room to eat in.*

LEFT ABOVE & BELOW *The house has views out over Strangford Lough towards Mid Island and the surrounding low-lying fields which flood after heavy rains.* OPPOSITE *Grey Abbey is built on one of the oldest parks in Ireland, which was laid out by Sir James Montgomery over the grounds of the old Cistercian settlement. The Palladian-style house was built in local stone.*

ABOVE *A collection of family portraits hangs in the entrance hall and on the walls of the gallery level above.* RIGHT *The cantilevered staircase with its sweeping curves and delicate proportions dates from the early nineteenth century. Built entirely of wood, it is considered a miracle that it stays up at all, and is so light that it seems to float around the hall.*

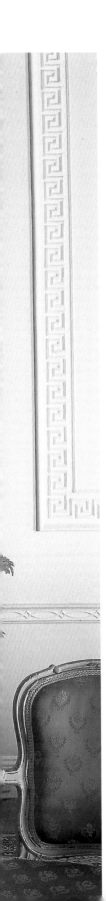

LEFT *An Irish sideboard, built for the original house in 1760, stands in an alcove which was decorated with plaster fleur-de-lys in anticipation of a visit from the Prince of Wales which never happened. The portrait above the sideboard is of John Charles Montgomery.* FAR LEFT *A portrait of William Montgomery, who built the first house in 1718, hangs above a Regency chaise longue in the Blue Drawing Room. Family lore has it that his glum expression is due to the envelope he holds, containing the bill for the house.*

RIGHT *The Middle Drawing Room is dominated by an 1840s Broadwood concert grand piano which Daphne bought at an auction for £25. It is covered with family photographs. A portrait of the daughter of Lord Peterborough hangs above the fireplace.* BELOW *An old album contains a photograph of the abbey ruins in the park of Grey Abbey, together with an extract from a family diary.*

ABOVE *Three doors lead from the Middle Drawing Room to the library,*
flower room and Gothic dining room, respectively. OPPOSITE *An elegant,*
carved Gothic hall chair announces the entrance to the Gothic dining
room, which William Montgomery added to the house as a drawing
room in the late 1700s, inspired by his wife's family seat, Castle Ward.

ANCESTRAL ESTATE

THE O'NEILLS ARE ONE OF THE TRADITIONAL IRISH CLANS AND ALLEGEDLY THE OLDEST TRACEABLE FAMILY IN EUROPE, WITH ESTATES THAT BEFORE THE LAND ACTS MUSTERED A QUARTER OF A MILLION ACRES. The family seat of the O'Neills had long been Shane's Castle on Lough Neagh, but in 1816 it accidentally burnt to the ground. The head of the northern branch of the O'Neills at the time, Earl O'Neill, decided against rebuilding the castle but instead built a number of different houses where he and his brother, both bachelors, could gamble and entertain their lady friends. Among the buildings was a lodge which served as the main residence, a picturesque eyebrow-thatched cottage *orné,* designed in the style of architect John Nash. It was constructed at Cleggan on land which had been mortgaged and lost by the O'Neill of the day to Lord Mountcashel in the early eighteenth century.

In 1895, the property returned to the family fold when the great-grandfather of the present Hugh O'Neill, now Lord Rathcavan, bought the Cleggan estate as his own property to take advantage of the miles of surrounding tundra and the good shooting. The lodge had fallen into disrepair, with cattle milling through the ruins of the downstairs rooms, so three new cottages were built along the drive where the shooting parties could overnight. It was not until 1927 when Hugh's grandfather took over the property that it was destined to become a family home.

There followed a frantic programme of restoration and rebuilding. A kitchen wing, bathrooms and an impressive double staircase were added, and what was left of the thatched roof of the original folly was replaced with fish-scale slates. Top-floor bedrooms were created with dormer gables. A cousin living with the family at the time, Major John

ABOVE *One of several Wedgwood plaques which decorate a marble fireplace in the drawing room.* OPPOSITE *A glimpse into one of the boys' bedrooms reveals a hammock slung across one corner of the room in front of the bookshelves displaying photographs and mementos.*

Torrens, supervised the restoration and installed a primitive hydro-electric system and a battery room which housed an amazing engine to generate electricity. He created a reservoir behind the hill to supply the lodge with mountain water, and a water garden and rock garden soon followed. The idea of a farm to support the estate was the next to take off, and gradually the family began to acquire a little more land.

Hugh O'Neill remembers a very happy childhood spent predominantly at Cleggan, where he stayed with his grandparents during World War II and for school holidays thereafter. His mother had abandoned the family for an ungallant colonel when Hugh was fifteen and from that time onwards his life seems to have revolved around the busy workings of the estate. He bought out his father's life interest in Cleggan in 1978, and started yet another fundamental stage of restoration on the lodge which, during the latter years of his grandfather's long tenure, had begun to deteriorate.

Hugh married his French wife Sylvie in 1983 and the modernisation of Cleggan has been going on ever since. With Hugh's appointment as chairman of the Northern Ireland Tourist Board in 1986, the family has been able to spend the best part of the last decade in Antrim, repairing outhouses, redesigning the gardens and restoring the cottages. Life at Cleggan has now achieved an organised rhythm. Its 1,000 acres support a farm of sheep and cattle, and the surrounding hills – from where the Western Isles of Scotland can be seen on a clear day – still echo with the noise of gunfire from organised shooting parties. There are now three holiday cottages available for letting throughout the year, as a base for touring the famous Glens of Antrim, just five miles away on the north coast, or simply as a place to get away from it all.

ABOVE *The spectacular double staircase which was added in 1927 maintains the symmetry of this former shooting lodge.*
OPPOSITE *A Victorian 'Irish Chippendale' sidetable with a marble top stands in the hallway, which divides the octagonal dining and drawing rooms.*

OVERLEAF *Cleggan Lodge stands on a wooded hillside looking across the Braid Valley to Slemish Mountain beyond.*

ABOVE & OPPOSITE *The symmetry of this beautiful house is illustrated not only in the architectural repetition of octagonally shaped rooms, but also in the way furniture and objects have been placed in each room. As this view towards the fireplace in the drawing room shows, a pair of ceramic vases, matching sidetables, lamps, paintings and even the individual objects on the mantelpiece create a mirror image.*

ABOVE *The octagonal shape of each of the main rooms at Cleggan is probably clearest of all in the master bedroom, which is situated above the drawing room and looks out over Fisher's Pond and the surrounding parkland.* LEFT *Across the main landing is the guest bedroom, which is dominated by a four-poster bed. The bed was bought in Ireland many years ago but had been abandoned by Hugh in an outbuilding until Sylvie discovered it one day and reappropriated it for the guest room.*

GEORGIAN COUNTRY

AN EXCITED MELEE OF DOGS SCRAMBLES FROM THE BACK OF AN ESTATE CAR ONTO THE GRAVEL DRIVE WHICH LEADS UP TO THE ELEGANT FRONT DOOR OF A DIGNIFIED GEORGIAN HOUSE. Someone appears from the back of the house and relieves the shooting party of its assorted spoils – it has been a reasonable day and the bag is 'tolerable'. Rain-soaked jackets and mud-spattered boots are littered about the vaulted entrance hall as the party pads into the drawing room for drinks before disappearing up to their rooms to soak away the day's exertions in a steaming bath.

It has been another perfect day for George Gossip, the tenant of Tullanisk, the beautiful dower house to Lord Rosse's Birr Castle in Co. Offaly, which he currently runs together with his wife Susie as a country house hotel. The couple came to Birr ten years ago looking for a house where the rooms were not so big that they would feel uncomfortable on their own, yet large enough that when the house was filled with guests there would be space for everybody.

Tullanisk met their needs exactly. It is a classical Georgian house, built in 1795 and refurbished in 1820, which stands in its own graceful park sheltered behind a discreet wall a few miles from Birr and the castle. The tall Georgian windows in the classical house provide unimpeded vistas of the Irish countryside: of the herds of wild fallow deer which come to graze on the sweet grass – a mass of self-seeded daffodils in spring; or of carpets of fragile snowdrops amid the patchy frost in January, when Tullanisk is at its most beautiful – a pastel grey house in a pale, wintry landscape.

The Gossips were entranced by both the beauty of Tullanisk and its location in the heart of the country, where shooting and fishing were a way of life. The couple had

ABOVE *A detail of the plaster-work in an alcove at one end of the dining room, which reads* 'credens adjuvor'.
OPPOSITE A *portrait of Sir John Newport, flanked by portraits of other family members, hangs above the circular fireplace in the dining room. One of only two such fireplaces in Ireland, the other is to be found at Trinity College in Dublin.*

realised that Tullanisk was not only classically beautiful from the outside, it also commanded splendid views encompassing the variety of the surrounding Irish country-side. Its proximity to an elegant Georgian town with a famous castle to attract hordes of foreign visitors was an additional bonus, and the prospects looked promising. Reluctant to sell his dower house, previously leased to Mariga Guinness, Lord Rosse felt it would be a good idea to make it pay for itself, and the opportunity for the Gossips to take it on and run Tullanisk as a small hotel was too good to pass up.

Over the eight years since the Gossips moved in, major improvements have taken place. A new roof was swiftly followed by the installation of central heating (which had been limited previously to the hall and basement), seven new bathrooms to augment the one solitary bathroom they had inherited, and new carpets and curtains.

Neither of them wanted the decoration of Tullanisk to look overdone, but set out to give the impression that the refurbishment had come together over a number of years. It is not furnished in any one style since many of the pieces originated at Tullanisk, supplemented by others from the couple's previous homes, but is influenced by Mariga Guinness' choice of strong colours in the dining room, entrance hall and reception rooms.

Motivated by a mutual desire to meet new people, the Gossips' foray into the hotel business has ensured that George spends as many days shooting as he could wish for. The area is abundant with snipe and woodcock, and shooting parties meet up regularly at Tullanisk. Many evenings now find friends mingling with paying guests over drinks in the drawing room before moving through to the candlelit dining room for a meal of game, which George has inevitably shot, and also probably cooked himself.

ABOVE *One of several guest bed-rooms, this one has a lace-covered bed and Gothic windows which look out over the parkland.* OPPOSITE *The wintry facade of Tullanisk viewed from across the park, which is dotted with clusters of fragile snowdrops.*

ABOVE *Victorian-style paper silhouettes hang above the fireplace in one*
of the bedrooms. In keeping with the strong colours used for many of
the rooms, the walls here were sponged by George Gossip with a mixture
of blues and violets. RIGHT *A low sofa sits against a wall of engravings*
in the large drawing room. The Gossips believe that it is not enough to
have a beautifully furnished house, but that each room should be
matched by wonderful views of the countryside.

RIGHT *The vaulted entrance hall with its classical Georgian door and fanlight echoes the architectural style of Birr Castle, seat of the Earls of Rosse since 1620.* OPPOSITE *A colourful kilim hangs at one end of the vaulted entrance hall. A plaster of Paris bust of a Tuareg warrior is highlighted between a pair of Irish eighteenth-century chairs.*

ABOVE LEFT *The upstairs landing is painted a striking yellow, the colour continuing down the curve of the modest stairwell.* ABOVE RIGHT *A view through the door into the Pink Bedroom, the walls decorated with watercolours painted by Susie Gossip's grandmother. The curtains are made of calico and painted with emulsion.* RIGHT *The only ground-floor bedroom features a Gothic dividing wall, designed to conceal a bathroom.*

TRIM

CAVAN

Roscom

NAUGHT

MON

Langford

E MEA

TRIM

MULLINGAR

W MEATH

WAY

ATHENNY

PHILIPSTOO

KINGS Cº

KIL

BAB

LARE

INIS

LEINST

MARYBOROUGH

ATHY

QUEENS

CO

CAP

KIL

LOW

ERICK

TIPPE

KEN

NY

CHAPTER TWO

TOWN & COUNTRY

DUN LAOGHAIRE • DUBLIN TOWN • HAMWOOD •
CO. KILDARE • LARCHILL • LISS ARD • ORMOND QUAY

SEASIDE SANCTUARY

ON THE DRIVE SOUTH ALONG THE COAST ROAD OUT OF DUBLIN, THE CITY APPEARS TO HAVE ABSORBED ALL THE ONCE-INDEPENDENT TOWNS AND VILLAGES ON ITS FRINGES. Among these is Dun Laoghaire, an insignificant harbour village in the eighteenth century, which grew in stature and importance between 1820 and 1870. The town's development was influenced in part by the construction of an artificial harbour for the mail and packet services to Holyhead, and specifically by the rail link out of Dublin in 1834, which brought the independent township significantly closer to the city. Dun Laoghaire became popular as a holiday retreat for Dublin's wealthy inhabitants, holiday villas were built along the coast and the town became increasingly fashionable as a locality for yacht racing and other seaside pastimes.

In 1846 a local architect decided to build a series of terraces, inspired by the coastal architecture of Italy. Money was to run out before he could complete his project, but the rows of houses which he did accomplish, following the contours of the bay, stand today as testimony to his vision. Painted in soft pastel shades, the houses look like cottages when approached from the road. However, a glimpse of the entire terrace from across the bay reveals in reality how much bigger they are, extending four storeys down the cliff, with terraced gardens of palm trees and exotic flowers descending to a stony beach and a small slipway. It is a wonderfully romantic location and the setting for a fascinating tale.

At the tender age of eighteen a young bride came to live as a tenant in one of the terrace houses, and was to stay there her entire life. When her husband died in middle age, she remained alone. She would be seen occasionally working in the steep garden, becoming increasingly eccentric and reclusive as time went by, until she refused to see

ABOVE *The front door still boasts its original brass lock and old-fashioned bell-pull.*
OPPOSITE *Glynis Robins has never liked dark mahogany furniture. Her husband, however, comes from a family of cabinet makers and his study is the one exception in this house of pale furnishings. An original black marble fireplace adds to the masculine image.*

visitors altogether. At the time, Glynis Robins and her husband were living in a mews house which had been sold to them by the owner of this partic- ular house in the terrace. Captivated by its position overlooking the sea and intrigued by the air of mystery which had surrounded the property for so many years, Glynis persuaded her husband to make discreet enquiries as to its availability. The initial answer was firmly negative, only for the owner to change her mind completely a few days later.

The couple bought the terrace without ever having set foot inside it, the one futile attempt they made at gaining entry having been rebuffed by the elderly incumbent. Glynis and her husband purchased the house on the understanding that they could not move in until the old lady had died. Three years later they crossed the threshold of their new home for the first time. The scene that greeted them was one of eccentric decay, a house in a state of complete neglect, its rooms clouded with years of cobwebs and dust.

The pale, almost Swedish style with which Glynis Robins has deftly transformed the interior of the house reflects a taste she has developed over the years in her small village shop The Dalkey Design Company. The rooms in the house are minimally yet comfortably furnished with bare wooden floorboards painted cream throughout. Huge floor-to-ceiling windows flood the south-facing rooms with light and look out over sweep- ing Killiney Bay and the terraced gardens below.

Although the couple have a holiday cottage on the coast of Connemara for long breaks away from Dublin, their romantic, light-filled house in Dun Laoghaire fulfils their need for a peaceful sanctuary away from the pressures of city life.

ABOVE *The sea is a constant and soothing presence. The view from the house is over Killiney Bay to the distant Sugar Loaf.* OPPOSITE *A wooden bowl filled with creamy shells, which were washed up on the beach one winter, brings a sense of the ocean inside. The sound of the waves crashing on the rocks below is always audible.*

ABOVE *The careful arrangement of delicate objects in the drawing room is indicative of Glynis Robins' style. The small sculpture on the mantelpiece is by her daughter, Alannah Robins.* RIGHT *The light, sun-drenched drawing room is simply furnished, its pale decoration lending it a Swedish feel – a far cry from the dark neglected interiors, complete with old gas fittings, which Glynis inherited.*

OPPOSITE *A wicker basket filled with the pale pink shells of sea urchins, collected near their holiday home in Connemara on the west coast of Ireland.* RIGHT The Fables of La Fontaine *lies open at 'The Little Fish and the Fisherman' on a reading stand attached to a comfortable armchair in one of the bedrooms.* BELOW RIGHT *The white and dusky blue of the bathroom echoes the calming colour scheme of the bedrooms.* BELOW *A rustic French bed in the master bedroom is washed in pale blue. The lace touches make this a very feminine room.*

ELEGANT ECCENTRIC

THE CLASSICALLY ELEGANT HOUSE OF WRITER POLLY DEVLIN STANDS IN ONE OF DUBLIN'S FAMED GEORGIAN TERRACES. It differs from its neighbours in one small detail; instead of a gravel parking bay outside it boasts a traditional garden and a flagstone path leading to the front door. Yet less than a decade ago it was a derelict tenement with an uncertain future.

ABOVE *An extensive collection of Staffordshire dogs is grouped together on a Chinese cabinet.* OPPOSITE *A tapestry surrounded by a collection of paintings hangs on one wall of the drawing room, with chairs squeezed either side of a lacquer table topped with framed photographs.*

Polly Devlin was born and grew up in Co. Tyrone in Northern Ireland and, like many in the literary circle of the time, enjoyed a romantic relationship with Dublin, hitchhiking to the capital with student friends to drink in its vibrant glamour. Firmly rooted in Ireland and yet never feeling quite at home, Polly travelled and lived in New York and Tuscany before settling in England, where she has a house in London and another in Somerset. Neither of these homes has stopped her feeling that, as a writer, she will always be restless, wanting to move on almost as soon as she has arrived.

In 1990, Polly's father died. Three weeks after the funeral she found herself sitting dismally in the empty house, where Willy, her father's old friend, was struggling to light a fire, rolling up pieces of old newspaper. On one of them Polly suddenly spotted a crude drawing of a house and the headline 'House for someone who wants to restore a beautiful building'. With no idea what prompted her and no clue as to where in Dublin this house might be, Polly reached for the telephone and dialled the agent. The property was due to be sold at auction at 2pm that afternoon.

Twenty minutes later, Polly found herself rattling down the main road on the three-hour journey to Dublin. She arrived at the derelict house only to realise that the auction was being held at a nearby hotel. She tore into the auction room just in time to

put in an offer against the highest bidder. The agent in charge had no idea who this wild woman was and he put down his gavel to check whether the vendors wished to go through with the offer, since he could not vouch for the stranger. His hesitation cost Polly since the underbidder in the meantime had screwed up sufficient courage to put in a counter bid, which she had to top. Polly nervously searched for her cheque-book as the agent approached her across the room to extract his deposit. All that remained was to be taken on a tour of her new property and to worry about where she would find the rest of the money.

The house was such a disaster that Polly left for London immediately, only returning ten days later to try and come to terms with what she had bought. It never occurred to her to sell the house. Whatever had taken hold and prompted her to buy it was still there. While her daughter celebrated her twenty-first birthday in Cambridge, Polly was camping in the front room of her tenement, bleakly surveying her new home – the rooms divided up into three flats, the damaged architectural details and cornices, the missing fireplaces and doors and the 1950s-style windows. Her thoughts were interrupted by a ring at the door. It was the underbidder from the auction.

Hoping to have purchased the property to do up and sell on, the underbidder knew the house well and offered to become her builder. They restored the basement first, turning it into a flat for Polly to live in while the rest of the house was in turmoil. Discovering she knew next to nothing about Dublin, Polly started work on a guide book to the city. Just as she got to know every stick and stone of Dublin, she also became familiar with her new house, literally peeling back the layers of history piece by piece.

ABOVE *A Gothic chair with a tapestry seat and back sits on the landing between two bedrooms. The Catholic figures were left on the chair accidentally one day and have stayed there ever since.*
OPPOSITE *A wall in one of Polly's rooms has almost disappeared behind a grandfather clock, a Chinese cabinet, paintings and other objects which cover it.*

ABOVE & RIGHT *Polly Devlin's Dublin home is like a stage set, a theatrical backdrop against which her life is enacted. Her two sitting rooms, which are connected with folding panelled doors, are filled to capacity with furniture and objects which she brought over in stages from England and does not remember actually buying. One exception is the blue and white china displayed in the green room – it is predominantly the work of Simon Petit who lived in London's Spitalfields.*

ABOVE & OPPOSITE *The mood of the guest bedroom is overwhelmingly romantic. The hand-blocked wallpaper, decked with numerous framed prints and paintings, reminded Polly of bedrooms she had slept in as a young girl. The four-poster is a Napoleonic campaign bed, which can be folded up and stored away if necessary.*

ABOVE *Polly makes a point of displaying unusual objects in unexpected places. In one corner of a bathroom is an antique embroidered fire screen, used by ladies to protect their complexions while sitting fireside.* RIGHT *The Victorian bath with its original taps and fittings was found in Ireland, and the French hand-blocked wallpaper is covered in framed antique tapestries and needlework.*

INTERIOR GILDING

THE ENTRANCE TO HAMWOOD IS AS INCONSPICUOUS AS THAT OF MANY A COUNTRY HOUSE IN IRELAND – A SIMPLE GATE SET BACK FROM THE ROAD, LOST IN THE LUSH GROWTH OF THE SURROUNDING RHODODENDRONS AND WOODLAND. Yet, tucked away just inside is a whitewashed Gothic gatehouse and a drive which meanders gently through the woods, the grass on either side sprinkled with blue Apennine anemones. Massive stumps are all that remain of once ancient trees at the approach to the garden, their decaying strength softened by yellow daffodils.

There is a simplicity about Palladian architecture which belies the perfect proportions of the houses built in this style. Hamwood, its exterior discoloured by years of wet winters, comprises a classical facade and two beautiful octagonal pavilions which are attached to the central house by a pair of curved wings at either side.

Home to the Hamilton family since 1779, very little appears to have changed in the ensuing 200 years since the first Charles Hamilton bought a farm and some land from the neighbouring estate and, with the help of a Dublin surveyor, Joseph O'Brien, erected a Palladian villa on the site in 1787 for a mere £2,500. Having established a reputation as an importer of fine wines, Charles Hamilton found himself appointed Land Agent to the Dukes of Leinster in 1798 to work the land, after a curious series of events.

Just as generations of Hamiltons have lived in the area, so too have descendants of other families. Among these are the Rileys, blacksmiths in the eighteenth century and blacksmiths still, who tell the story of how their ancestor saved Charles Hamilton from the scaffold which was awaiting him in Dunboyne during an uprising. As he was marched off to his fate by the rebels, Riley addressed the crowd, implying that the

ABOVE *An ornate original door plate, handle and lock on one of the drawing room doors.*
OPPOSITE *Above a simple marble fireplace in the drawing room hangs an elaborate gilt-edged mirror and a collection of framed miniatures and photographs.*

condemned man would be of more use alive than dead. His life was spared, although the Duke of Leinster's agent at the time was less fortunate. On his execution the appointment was offered to Charles Hamilton. The position has stayed in the family ever since.

The present generation of Hamiltons to enjoy Hamwood, the sixth to be called Charles, and his wife Anne, have lived in the house since 1961 and quite obviously adore the place. Family memorabilia, each piece with a story to tell, has its place in the scheme of things. Tables and other surfaces are filled with photographs, while several ancestral paintings in large gilt frames grace the terra-cotta walls of the magnificent dining room. Some were painted by another member of the family, Eva Hamilton, who was a pupil of Orpen (one of Ireland's best known portrait painters), and whose prodigious talent is greatly in evidence throughout the house.

Another lady of the house who contributed significantly to the overall look and comfort of the interior was Caroline Tighe, wife of the second Charles Hamilton, whose ideas on decoration have remained largely unchallenged to this day.

Since most of the furniture was designed for the house, there is very little scope for rearranging the rooms and the most recent change to the overall plan was in the drawing room, formerly the music room. The original moss green walls were universally faded so whenever a painting or object was moved, a dark green patch was revealed. Charles and Anne took the difficult decision to redo the walls, and chose a soft blue-green, which creates a perfect backdrop for the gilt framed pictures and musical motifs which adorn the room. The result is a room of extraordinary beauty, with several of the paintings rehung and smaller objects repositioned. Caroline Tighe would doubtless have approved.

ABOVE *A photograph of Anne Hamilton, aged four, and one of husband Charles at thirty-five – two of many family photographs displayed throughout the house – are propped up on a desk against a shelf of leather-bound books.*
OPPOSITE *Charles and Anne Hamilton replaced the original dark green of the drawing room with a delicate blue-green.*

ABOVE *The large double drawing room was originally the music room and a grand piano still takes pride of place.* LEFT *Portraits, drawings and silhouettes blend with vases and miniatures, ornamental shelves of ceramics, and gilded musical motifs to create a sense of genteel elegance.*

RIGHT *The entrance hall is in one of the octagonal pavilions that flank the house. The wall is hung with six pictures depicting the Duke of Wellington's funeral.* OPPOSITE *The two curved wings and octagonal pavilions were added to the house five years after the Hamiltons first moved in. The draughts were so bad in the drawing room that the lady of the house insisted the outside door be moved further away. The stained pine panelling came from Memel in Russia, and the floor is laid with Victorian tiles.*

OVERLEAF *Hamwood was named after the union of a Hamilton with a Chetwood. Many of the trees in the grounds came as cuttings from the Duke of Leinster's plantation at the Carton Estate.*

EARTHLY PLEASURES

A SOLITARY FISH JUMPS IN THE STILL WATERS OF THE GRAND CANAL, MOMENTARILY BREAKING THE OILY SURFACE AND SENDING A SUCCESSION OF SLOW RIPPLES TO LOSE THEMSELVES IN THE REEDS AND GRASSES THAT FRINGE THE MUDDY BANKS. In the distance, beyond the gaunt branches of the wintry trees dotting the countryside, the grey facade of a classical Georgian house can be glimpsed. Its position on a knoll above the canal affords a view down the length of the waterway as it winds its way from the River Shannon towards Dublin.

Situated in Co. Kildare – the heart of Ireland's horse-breeding and racing country – the handsome house is fittingly surrounded by rolling fields that are home to a growing number of fine racehorses. A brand new, horseshoe-shaped stable block stands testimony to the passion which Ronnie Wood, guitarist with the Rolling Stones, has been pursuing for the last ten years. A betting man since his childhood days, when his father would send him down to the bookmakers, Ronnie Wood's own horses are now winning races for him – a thrill he has not yet quite got used to.

At the entrance to the property, a surprisingly grand pair of wrought-iron gates open noiselessly at a car's approach. A new drive has just been laid and the smell of tar is still heavy in the air. It circumnavigates the old garden wall which encloses the house, and links it to the new stable complex and a large free-standing building where Ronnie's wife Jo has created an exotic pool house. Inside, an Olympic-sized swimming pool unfolds, with medieval-style candelabra hanging overhead, long draperies at the full-length windows and Indian chairs creating a magical envrionment where the couple can unwind after horse training, or even after a long period away from home on tour.

ABOVE *A portrait of fellow Rolling Stone, Charlie Watts, painted by Ronnie Wood.* OPPOSITE *In the private pub, a suit of armour clutching a pint of Guinness stands beside an antique throne – just two items in a random collection which Ronnie Wood has accumulated during his travels.*

ABOVE *Beyond the house, the Grand Canal meanders across the Irish countryside between the River Shannon and Dublin.* OPPOSITE *The grey Georgian house would once have been approached from this side, as the simple stone steps to the front door indicate. However, the drive now turns into the courtyard at the back of the property, which is enclosed by a high garden wall.*

The house itself backs on to a gravelled courtyard, around which random outbuildings and the original stables have been given a new lease of life. The modest size of the house has meant that Ronnie's hobbies are fostered beyond the walls of the family home which he shares with Jo and their four children. A sound-proof recording studio has been built into the old stable block, where the Stones have been known to practise, while the far end of the stables has been given over to Ronnie's other interest – painting. Portraits of horses, friends and members of the band decorate the walls, while other half-finished canvases are propped up on easels.

Across the courtyard is the pub, Yer Father's Yacht, with a portrait of Ronnie's father on the inn sign above the inscription 'Purveyor of fine wines, beers and spirits (for absolutely nothing)'. The pub is dominated by a huge billiard table where Ronnie, who is snooker-crazy, has regular matches with friend and fellow Londoner, Jimmy White. The rough, whitewashed walls are crowded with pictures and photographs, the pine-clad ceiling is dotted with assorted beer mats tacked in place, and the room is filled with trophies and memorabilia which Ronnie has picked up on his travels around the world. A fully equipped bar and a colourful juke box at the opposite end of the room testify to the hours spent in this atmospheric and hedonistic playhouse.

While Ronnie is busy with the horses or caught up in one of his many pastimes, Jo takes care of the estate. On tour with Ronnie for much of the time, she has had little opportunity to explore her interest in interior design. Already, though, the couple have managed to create an extraordinary private world – a secluded setting, a successful stable of race horses, and all the diversions a rock-and-roll star could wish for.

OPPOSITE *Jo Wood has painted the drawing room a deep blue, creating a suitably bold backdrop for the marble fireplace, gilt mouldings and one of Ronnie's Gibson guitars.* BELOW LEFT & RIGHT *Despite the occasional rock-and-roll touches, the overall mood of the house is one of elegance and tradition. A pair of antique dolls sit beneath a portrait among other objects on a chest of drawers in the master bedroom; and a classical harp is displayed on the landing of the simple central staircase.*

LEFT *Ronnie Wood indulges his passion for painting in the stable block which forms part of the courtyard at the back of the house. A portrait of one of his horses is in progress on the easel, one of Keith Richards stands on the mantelpiece and others of Mick Jagger and the band are propped up on the floor.*

ABOVE *A pair of Indian chairs inlaid with mother-of-pearl and situated at one end of the pool.* RIGHT *The enormous swimming pool is the result of a confusion on the construction plans between feet and metres. Hence an expanse of water of Olympic proportions, framed by a slate floor and surrounded by hammocks and groups of comfortable chairs.*

LEFT & BELOW *A fantasy world that would be the envy of many men, Ronnie's pub, Yer Father's Yacht, features a well-stocked bar and a huge billiard table. Music is generated on a colourful Wurlitzer jukebox at the far end of the room. Ronnie has personalised his private tavern with an eccentric collection of objects, paintings, photographs and beer mats.*

FOLLY GRANDEUR

A PLUME OF SMOKE RISES THROUGH THE DARK LARCH TREES IN A DISTANT CORNER OF THE ESTATE WHERE MICHAEL DE LAS CASAS IS CUTTING BACK THE UNDERGROWTH, ENGROSSED IN TENDING HIS BONFIRE, WHILE UP AT THE HOUSE, THE ORNATE IRON GATES AND RAILINGS SURROUNDING THE PROPERTY ARE BEING GIVEN A FRESH COAT OF PAINT. There is quiet activity almost everywhere, except in the farmyard where several rare breeds of pig are stretched out in their pen soaking up an afternoon of unexpected sunshine. A typical country scene perhaps, but Larchill is no ordinary farm.

When Michael and his wife Louisa first discovered the property in 1994 they had no idea that the dilapidated park concealed an eighteenth-century garden of remarkable follies and waterways – probably the only one of its kind still existing in the world today. The existence of this 'Sleeping Beauty' was revealed by garden historian Patrick Bowes, who came to lunch one day about six months after the family had moved in, and realised what lay within the grounds. He urged them to restore the lost arcadia.

The origins of the garden remain a mystery. All that is known is that it was built by a family by the name of Prentice, wealthy haberdashers who owned considerable amounts of land in the area, on which they grew flax for linen and built their mills, and who acquired the demesne of Phepotstown at the beginning of the eighteenth century. Larchill formed part of the property, and its development as a *ferme ornée*, literally an 'ornamented farm', is the subject of much conjecture. The Prentices may have been inspired by the temples, pagodas and gardens of the Far East, where they traded. They also had a town house in Laracor next to Jonathan Swift, who was vicar there at the time, and there is speculation that they supplied Swift, who was passionately interested in

ABOVE *One of the stained glass windows in the Shell Tower was copied from the original by artist Michael Judd. The thick tower walls are encrusted with shells.* OPPOSITE *A narrow set of stairs wind up inside the Shell Tower, a three-storey crenellated folly built into the garden wall.*

fermes ornées, with his finery in exchange for advice and ideas. More likely, though, is that they were simply keeping up with their neighbour, the Earl of Mornington, who had created over 100 acres of lakes and islands on his estate, including an island fort called Gibraltar, where mock naval battles would be enacted. Lending credence to this idea is the existence of a similar island fort called Gibraltar at Larchill.

Whether as a direct result of their *folie de grandeur* or not, in 1780 the Prentices were declared bankrupt and Larchill was acquired by the Watsons, who planted over 25,000 trees during the century in which the property remained with the family. Described as 'the most fashionable garden in all of Ireland' in notes to an Ordnance Survey map of 1836, Larchill and its follies had sunk without trace by the middle of the twentieth century. The walls were either in ruins or were completely overgrown; the park had been trampled by cattle, while the lake had completely disappeared.

With the help of various grants and architect James Howley, Michael and Louisa threw themselves into a four-year restoration. Michael was soon fascinated by the quirky follies, and even added a few of his own. Gradually, along with the restoration came an idea for a rare breeds farm, and Michael's pigs now luxuriate in a neo-Gothic folly of their own, while the goats inhabit a temple next door and the hens scratch about in the restored Gothic farmyard located close to the house.

There is a terrific sense of theatre about Larchill. The project to restore a unique collection of extraordinary buildings, and then to combine them with an eccentric menagerie of animals ensures endless surprises. A llama walking leisurely through a field of sheep, with the island fort of Gibraltar as a backdrop, says it all.

ABOVE *Rose, the family's Jack Russell, admires the view of the Wicklow Mountains from the front door of the farmhouse.* OPPOSITE *The interior of the house is warm and comfortable. The dining room walls are deep red, echoing the golden hue of the aged wooden floor.*

RIGHT & FAR RIGHT *The figure of Bacchus rises from the lake, traversed at one end by a small stone bridge.* OPPOSITE *The view from an upstairs window takes in the park and lake, with Fort Gibraltar in the middle, and the Wicklow Mountains beyond.* BELOW *Gibraltar, the restored folly in the centre of the lake, which the locals insist on referring to as 'the pond'. Michael de las Casas became engrossed in Larchill's quirky buildings and was intrigued by the madness which inspired such follies.*

LEFT & BELOW *Supposedly the first of the many follies to have been built, the restored Gothic farmyard close to the house now supports a wonderful variety of hens, peacocks, ducks and geese.* OPPOSITE *The functional but cosy kitchen where family life revolves around the Aga. A shelf suspended across the tiled alcove displays a collection of assorted teacups, mugs, jugs and plates.*

ABOVE *The walls of the spartan Victorian bathroom, with its wooden floor, have been given thick pink and white stripes.* OPPOSITE *The solid master bed was designed and built by Michael from huge heavy gate posts. The Gothic-style headboard was a later addition. The deeply recessed windows look out across the farm to the Wicklow Mountains.*

SPATIAL PURITY

VEITH TURSKE IS A DESIGNER OF ARCHITECTURE, INTERIORS AND LANDSCAPES, AND A MAN WHOSE PHILOSOPHY AND OUTLOOK ON LIFE INFLUENCE HIS WORK AND THE PEOPLE AROUND HIM ON A DAILY BASIS. He is also a man with a mission, and for the last decade has devoted himself to an extraordinary corner of west Cork, where he considers himself fortunate enough to have found a relatively untouched indigenous landscape. At Liss Ard, sixty acres which once formed part of the O'Donovan estates, Veith is gradually developing an ecologically designed Irish park.

Following the Land Reform Act of 1922, the estate had fallen on hard times. The two buildings it supported – a large Georgian house and a Victorian lodge – were little more than ruins when Veith and his wife Claudia decided to buy the property in 1989. Of the many gardens they had looked at all the way round the coast from Wicklow to Sligo, the one at Liss Ard with its diversity of meadows and woodland, a lake and numerous streams came closest to Veith's vision – although he was nearly too late. The eco-structure of Lough Abisdealy was in immediate danger, its water overwhelmed by the sewage and nitrates pouring in from the surrounding farmland, and Veith had to apply himself instantly to limiting the potential damage.

Restoring the buildings was secondary to Veith's overriding desire to save the gardens and he spent the first two years simply analysing what he had inherited to ensure he fully understood the ecosystem and could bring it back into balance. This period spent in the study and contemplation of the garden had already excited media attention as well as interest from well-respected garden foundations. In defining the garden, Veith was quickly forced into making a decision about the houses. As experts

ABOVE *The view through the circular window on the main staircase of the Georgian house.* OPPOSITE *An original green marble fireplace was retained in the Georgian house. The room, now made over into the dining room of this luxury hotel, is furnished with plain wooden tables and chairs in loose linen covers.*

and public alike began to show an interest in Liss Ard, Veith was in the process of restoring the large late-Georgian house where he and the family would live. Soon, they had all sorts of visitors looking for somewhere to stay and the idea of setting up a small luxury hotel was born.

The Lake Lodge was the obvious location. Used as a summer pavilion by the big house, its cramped late-Victorian proportions were completely reworked around Veith's idea that each of the rooms should be designed with the square as its basic unit, the purest possible design element. They are minimally furnished, with few, if any, pictures on the walls, and the beds are located in the centre of each room with a clear view out through large windows to the lake and gardens below. Combined with natural materials such as paper and wood, as well as the special relationship that the rooms enjoy with the garden, the interiors have a distinctly Japanese feel. They are also tranquil and calming, each room influenced by subtle differences in colour scheme, and by the play of light as it changes from dawn through dusk.

ABOVE *Among Veith's collection of books are Alfred Kubin's* Zwölf Frühe Blätter *and* A Still Life of Sigmund Freud. OPPOSITE *The drawing room is furnished in a minimal style with contemporary sofas and armchairs grouped by a large bay window overlooking the garden.*

The transformation of the Georgian house was an easier proposition, its gracefully proportioned rooms and high ceilings more appropriate to Veith's spatial interpretation of a luxury hotel. However, he realised that the hotel was never going to be a commercial solution to looking after the garden and decided to transfer two-thirds of it – over forty acres – to the Liss Ard Foundation, a charity founded in 1990 to manage and maintain the Liss Ard garden. The remaining twenty acres are leased to the hotel and Veith hopes he has now established a peaceful coexistence between the hotel and foundation which will help to safeguard this unique piece of Ireland for the foreseeable future.

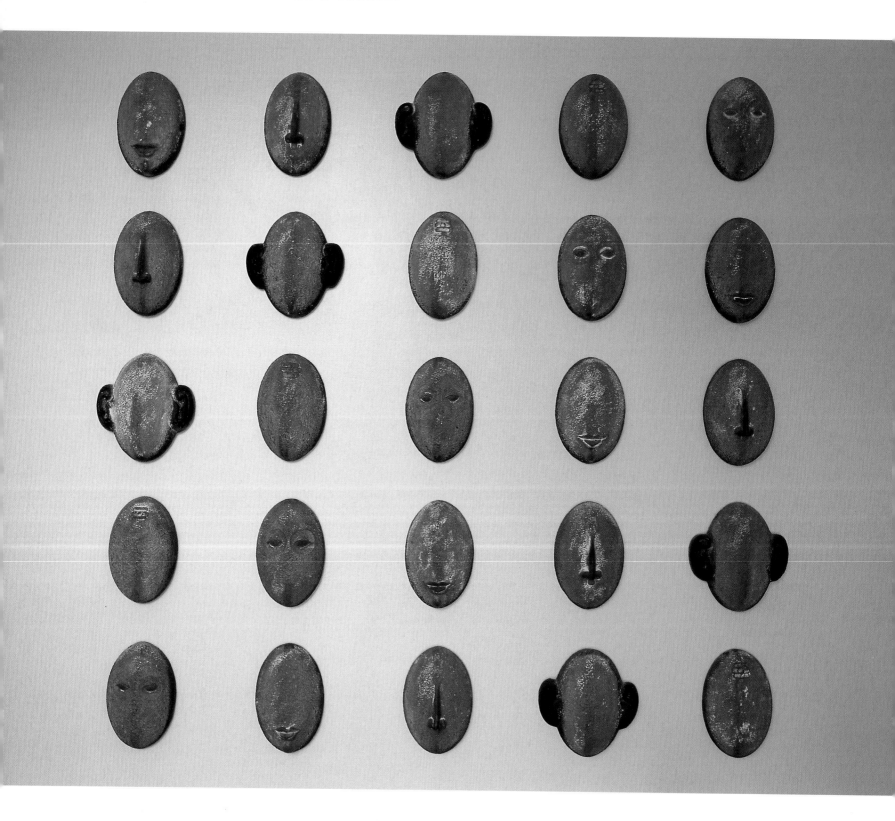

ABOVE *While in the bedrooms artworks are banished from the walls,*
they do appear in the communal living areas. The dining room is domin-
ated by five paintings by Stephen Cox, ovals of different colours, which
represent Water, Fire, Earth, Ether and Air. OPPOSITE *A collection of*
masks on the wall of the main corridor is also by artist Stephen Cox.

ABOVE LEFT & RIGHT *The attraction of Liss Ard is its pristine setting –*
the waters of Lough Abisdealy ripple in the breeze, and a fine rain mists
the view of Lake Lodge from the old wooden jetty. RIGHT *The view from*
the window of a bedroom in the Lake Lodge looks down over Lough
Abisdealy and on to the blue mountains of Kerry in the far distance.

LEFT *The bedrooms in the Lake Lodge are designed around the simplest of architectural forms – the square. Elements such as paper, wood and slate give the rooms a Japanese feel.* BELOW *Platforms provide accommodation for an additional mattress, located in some rooms above the sitting area and in others above the bathroom, which is concealed behind Japanese-style sliding wood and paper panels.*

ABOVE *In keeping with the all-white interiors of the Georgian house, the bathrooms in this part of the hotel are clad in white tiles, with large mirrors enhancing the sense of space.* RIGHT *Bathrooms in the Lake Lodge are more contemporary in style, with slate and chrome twin washbasins reflecting the Japanese style of the bedrooms.*

DUBLIN MODERN

NUMBER SIX ORMOND QUAY IS ONE OF THE FIVE OLDEST HOUSES IN DUBLIN. Built in 1684 by Sir Robert Doyne, Secretary to the Privy Council, as part of the embankment of Dublin's first quays, the house looks out over the Liffey, which flows through the heart of the city. Inhabited by merchants for two centuries, the property had fallen into decline in modern times, unable to withstand the thunder of traffic along the quay or the wave of indiscriminate building development which has gripped Dublin over the last few decades. By 1992 permission had been given to pull down all but the facade of the seventeenth-century house. It was then that Michael Smith, chairman of the Dublin City Association of An Taisce, the National Trust for Ireland, stepped in to rescue it from the demolition squad. Together with Ian Lumley, Director of Projects for the Dublin Civic Trust, Michael bought the historic house.

ABOVE *An elegant example of Dublin's architectural legacy: classical Georgian doorways with fanlights set above them.* OPPOSITE *A view of the Liffey which flows through central Dublin from the upstairs window of the house on Ormond Quay.*

His plan of salvage has been as multi-layered as the structure of the house proved to be. Its slow restoration has provided a unique insight into how the property would have evolved over the years. Originally a Dutch Billy, or gabled building, it was greatly altered over the years like many houses of its age. In the early eighteenth century, the first-floor front room was raised and the panelling from that room moved into the room above. In the late eighteenth or early nineteenth century, the gable structure was eliminated, and by the mid nineteenth century a shopfront had been inserted and the front wall rebuilt with the number of bays reduced from three to two.

Michael carried out emergency repairs and structural work immediately after his purchase and began by renovating the top two floors. Of the opinion that architects tend to have the wrong approach in their treatment of old buildings, he designed the quirky

features that distinguish his home with the help of a conservation engineer. Much of the top floor had been burnt in a fire in 1971 and Michael restored it with a philosophy of minimal intervention. Where interior fragments remained they were fixed; where they had been destroyed, an assertive contemporary approach was employed. The result is a space which has been refurbished in an aggressively modern fashion; the removal of the attic floor allows double-height ceilings. Working with what they had, the pair used salvage material wherever possible – a storage rack found in a skip, shutters created from timber boards and other ingenious forms of recycling.

Elsewhere, the general approach has been a careful restoration of all the existing features of age, while at the same time preserving intact the complex architectural layering of the four centuries since the property was built. Considerable attention has been paid to reinstating and restoring panelling and mouldings where once they should have been. Existing floorboards were kept and matched with others that were salvaged, and the nineteenth-century shuttered windowcases were restored.

By the time Number Six Ormond Quay is completely restored, the paintwork will have been conserved and cleaned, and joinery, plaster and decorative finishes will be reinstated, with some unrestored areas of brickwork, masonry, timber, paintwork and wallpaper left to show the complexity of the archaeological layering. Perhaps in response to Michael's extraordinary commitment to the property and his obsession with restoring every historical idiosyncrasy, the house was declared a National Monument in 1996. For Michael, though, it is still very much a family home.

ABOVE *Contemporary blue and red cabinets alongside glass shelves and metal racks are used for kitchen storage.*
OPPOSITE *In rooms where the original architectural features had disappeared, Michael let his imagination loose. For the open-plan kitchen he created a deeply scalloped work surface topped with bold blue tiles.*

RIGHT *Removing the attic allowed for a double-height conversion of the top floor of the property, which combines an open-plan living and kitchen area. Behind the modern shelving and fireplace, the bricks of the original chimney are revealed.* OPPOSITE *A steep metal ladder leads down from the bedroom which is built into the apex of the roof on a gallery level.*

RIGHT *The open-plan living area features floorboards painted white and is minimally furnished with a couple of white sofas and a black leather armchair.*
OPPOSITE *The metal ladder which ascends to the bedroom also serves as a divider between the kitchen and sitting room.*
BELOW *Mixing old and new, a period wrought-iron stove is set into a contemporary fireplace.*

GALWAY

GALWAY

ATHENRY

GALWAY BAY

CLARE

ENNIS

SHANNON R.

LIMERICK

MUNSTER

TRALEE

KER

L. LARNEY

CORK

TIPPE

RARY.

CLONMEL

WATERFO

KINGS C

PHILIPSTO

L E I N

MARYBORO

QUEE

CO

KI

KI

CHAPTER THREE

RUSTIC WAYS

North Antrim · Cill Rialaig · Leap Castle · Shanagarry ·
Spiddal · The Burren · Skibbereen

FARM COTTAGE

A THIN SPIRAL OF SMOKE DRIFTS FROM THE STONE CHIMNEY OF THE LARGER OF TWO COTTAGES TUCKED AWAY AGAINST THE DARKNESS OF THE HILL. The small yard, enclosed by a dry stone wall, is green with dripping moss, and the neighbouring fields are cropped by sheep. The ground on this still winter's day is hard and unyielding after last night's freeze. It is a perfect day for shooting.

As the sounds of gunfire carry across the hill, preparations for lunch are well underway in the main cottage. A delicious smell of lamb stew wafts from the stove, combining with the unmistakable scent of peat from the fireplace in the living room. Here, a long wooden table has been simply laid for the shooting party, which interrupts the quiet pastoral scene in a long trailer pulled by a noisy tractor, accompanied by a team of excited, if exhausted dogs. As the men gather around the table and the first bottle is broached, conversation turns to the quality of the morning's bag. The host of today's shoot, Hugh O'Neill, draws up a chair to the peat fire, much as all those years ago, the last owner of this farm, Jimmy Mann, might have done, warming his outstretched hands.

Old Jimmy Mann, as he was known to Hugh when a boy, is remembered as a rather spooky character, permanently dressed in a black suit and wearing a black hat pulled down low over his face. Mann's Farm represents a typical slice of social and economic history in north Antrim, a tiny farm of no more than fourteen acres and originally part of the O'Neill estates until it was bought out by the Land Acts about 1870. The Mann family would probably have been tenants.

The small stone cottage was the original building on the farm and dates from the sixteenth century. It was known as a byre dwelling. The family would have lived and

ABOVE *Typical of other such rural Irish properties, a dry stone wall encircles the farmstead.*
OPPOSITE *An old iron kettle and other utensils are kept close to the heat of a low peat fire where the day-to-day cooking would once have been carried out.*

slept in the loft, and cooked over the open peat fire among the animals on the stone floor below. The earliest survey of 1830 already shows the existence of the second, much larger dwelling and it seems extraordinary that such a small piece of land could have supported the luxury of two properties. Despite the presence of the larger cottage, life on the farm was extremely simple, even in Jimmy Mann's time. Meals were cooked over the fire, and a dark pot of soup and potatoes was a permanent fixture above the smoking peat. The farm produced flax and potatoes and probably supported a cow and a handful of sheep.

Old Jimmy Mann died intestate and for twelve years or more the farm was abandoned. By this time a near ruin, it was eventually sold to Hugh O'Neill, to whose family estate it had once belonged, and who had always loved its situation and the child-hood memories associated with it. Hugh became involved with the Tourist Board in 1986 and realised that, unlike Scotland and Wales, Northern Ireland did not cater for holiday cottage lettings. To sell the idea to the local sceptics, Hugh restored Mann's Farm as a prototype, leaving the beamed ceiling and peat fire in the main living room, converting bedrooms under the eaves, and replacing Old Jimmy Mann's unused parlour with a modern kitchen and a bathroom. The original byre dwelling was converted into a wonderfully romantic bedroom with a peat fire. The small wooden door opens out onto the yard and uninterrupted views over to the foothills of Slemish Mountain.

Thanks in part to Hugh's sensitive conversion, there are over 100 cottages which now participate in the letting scheme. With shooting parties during the winter months, and tourists through the short summer, Mann's Farm is rarely empty nowadays. Would Old Jimmy Mann recognise his home if he ever returned?

ABOVE *The decoration of the cottage is little changed – a few simple objects line the long wooden shelf above the fire.*
OPPOSITE *Peat from the bogs fuels the fire in the main parlour, where a table has been laid for lunch, its warmth welcoming the shooting party in from the surrounding woods.*

LEFT & BELOW *The byre dwelling has been sensitively restored and the interior transformed into an imaginative bedroom with a gallery. A peat fire is an almost constant feature of the original stone fireplace and chimney.*
OPPOSITE *After the main cottage was built, the byre dwelling nearby was used to house the animals.*

RIGHT *The farm cottages open out onto a yard, enclosed by a dry stone wall, with unhindered views to Slemish Mountain.*
BELOW *The woodlands in this corner of Antrim provide great opportunities for field sports. Hugh regularly organises shoots for friends and guests.*

COMMUNITY SPIRIT

CILL RIALAIG IS A MERE CLUSTER OF TINY STONE COTTAGES, ONE OF THE FURTHERMOST POINTS OF HABITATION IN CO. KERRY ON THE WEST COAST OF IRELAND, WHICH CLINGS TO THE EDGE OF THE CLIFF ON BOLUS HEAD HIGH ABOVE THE ATLANTIC OCEAN AND BALLINSKELLIGS BAY. Built about 1790, the eleven cottages which make up this isolated hamlet have withstood the relentless pounding of the elements through the centuries as rain and winds have gradually taken their toll.

The landscape is beautiful, rugged and demanding. The rocky terrain and spectacular cliffs, with views out to Scariff Island and the distant Skelligs, are resonant of an early mysticism which encouraged many to seek out this wild, unforgiving countryside and pit themselves against it. A line of megaliths leading up to Bolus Head, and the ruins of a hermitage beyond the village, stand testimony to those who went before.

Yet there are also survivors from the days when Cill Rialaig was still a struggling community. A glimpse of Mrs Kelly, comfortable in the passenger seat of a modern jeep as she is ferried to the local town a good distance away, brings the story right up to date for she was the last to vacate the hamlet back in the 1950s. Now she lives in a modern bungalow as close as possible to her old home, which, like so many of the other cottages, finally descended into ruin. But recently, Mrs Kelly has witnessed the unthinkable – the extraordinary restoration of her village by Noelle Campbell-Sharp, a successful publisher from Dublin, under the sensitive stewardship of friend and architect Alfred Cochrane.

The latest chapter in Cill Rialaig's fascinating history began when Noelle first visited the area over a decade ago and, like many before her, was captivated by the view and the stubborn tenacity of its inhabitants. Not far from the hamlet she bought a pair of

ABOVE *The conversion of the cowshed and two cottages into a single house has managed to incorporate the irregularities of the original stone walls.* OPPOSITE *A simple iron chair of contemporary French design sits against the slate-grey wall of the 'sky room' – in essence a stone corridor with a glazed glass roof – which links the two parts of Noelle Campbell-Sharp's home.*

old ruined cottages and cowshed from two elderly sisters, who agreed to sell only after she promised to respect its simple vernacular architecture.

As Noelle's own house began to take shape she found herself becoming increasingly involved with the local community and absorbed with the idea of rekindling life into the abandoned clifftop village. With the help of friends, a small Lottery grant and a wealth of enthusiasm, Noelle bought the collection of tumbledown cottages in 1991, and with Alfred Cochrane has been gradually restoring them.

The purpose behind Noelle's project was to create a new and thriving artistic community at Cill Rialaig, drawing on the unique spirit of the hamlet to attract artists and writers to spend a month at a time in relative isolation in one of the cottages, where they can work without being disturbed. In exchange for this unusual accommodation, which is offered without charge, each artist leaves behind something which they have produced during the month of their sojourn. This can then be sold to raise funds to continue the restoration work. The idea has proved extremely popular; the unique quality of light in this far-flung outpost of Ireland is attracting artists of international repute to take up Noelle's offer of hospitality.

Whether there will ever be sufficient funds to restore the entire village is a moot point. However, Noelle's efforts to date have been greeted with enthusiastic support by the locals. As guest of honour at a party to celebrate the completion of the first two cottages one summer's evening, Mrs Kelly recalled the last time she had had cause to dance in the village – when a barrel of rum came in on the waves over sixty years ago.

TOP & ABOVE *The views from Cill Rialaig's remote coastline are spectacular, whether the ruins of a keep, or out over Ballinskelligs Bay towards Scariff Island.*
OPPOSITE *Two of the hamlet's eleven cottages have so far been completed, one thatched and the other with a slate roof. They stand on opposite sides of the steep, rutted track which climbs up to Cill Rialaig.*

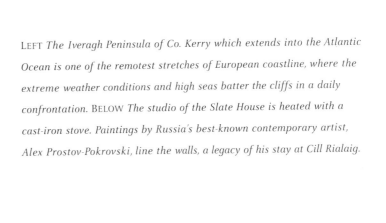

LEFT *The Iveragh Peninsula of Co. Kerry which extends into the Atlantic Ocean is one of the remotest stretches of European coastline, where the extreme weather conditions and high seas batter the cliffs in a daily confrontation.* BELOW *The studio of the Slate House is heated with a cast-iron stove. Paintings by Russia's best-known contemporary artist, Alex Prostov-Pokrovski, line the walls, a legacy of his stay at Cill Rialaig.*

ABOVE LEFT & RIGHT *The rugged exterior of Noelle's house, which was restored and adapted by architect Alfred Cochrane. The idea was to retain the original stone walls and remain as true as possible to the vernacular architecture of the area.* OPPOSITE *A peat fire next to a small cast-iron oven warms Noelle's cosy sitting room.*

LEFT *At one end of the sitting room, a wall of what locals refer to as 'keeping holes' is used for storing books. A ladder leads up to a small sleeping loft.*
OPPOSITE *A collection of Iveragh ceramics by Bob Hollis.*

ABOVE *A decorative late-Victorian fireplace at the end of the bed appears an unusually elegant feature in so isolated a cottage.* RIGHT *Noelle's bedroom is decorated in pale shades of blue. A rustic patchwork quilt covers the bed, swirling blue watercolours decorate the walls and pale saris filter the northern light that streams in through small windows.*

CASTLE KEEP

SEAN RYAN PLAYS THE PENNY WHISTLE. A COMBINATION OF TRADITIONAL IRISH MUSIC AND HIS OWN HAUNTING COMPOSITIONS, WHETHER ACCOMPANIED BY FRIENDS IN LOCAL BARS OR AT CEILIDHS, HAS GAINED HIM AN INTERNATIONAL REPUTATION AS A MUSICIAN. His head is filled with stories which have been passed down over the centuries in the form of songs, the old-fashioned way of keeping in touch with the local heritage of which the Irish are so fiercely proud. His wife Anne is a well-known Irish dancer and their daughter Ciara is following in her mother's footsteps.

As a family, the Ryans are touched with a romantic streak, a love of old buildings, and a fascination with the sense of history and untold tales locked within their thick walls. They had been renovating an old Church of Ireland rectory when a rumour reached them that nearby Leap Castle was to be put up for sale. They had barely a day to make up their minds before the property officially came onto the market. Anne had always wanted a castle, but what they bought was a ruin on a massive scale, a restoration project which will probably take them the rest of their lives to complete.

The Leap stands sentinel on the border between the counties of Offaly and Tipperary, looking out over rich farmland and a river valley to the Slieve Bloom Mountains beyond. In the gathering gloom of early evening it has a forbidding air, the crenellated walls which surround the property overgrown with grass and ivy. The keep is an ominous black silhouette. One of two Gothic wings which were added in the mid eighteenth century has tumbled into ruin, its walls blackened by fire.

The Ryans have moved mountains since they first became involved with The Leap, restoring the castle by slow degrees as time and money have afforded. Little remained of

ABOVE *The Leap of O'Banan (Leim-ui-Bhanain) was an ancient stronghold of the O'Carroll chieftains. Legend is divided as to the origin of its name. Popular local myth relates that two brothers came upon a rocky outcrop and decided that whoever survived after leaping to the ground far below should build a fortress.* OPPOSITE *A baronial fireplace dominates the vast entrance hall, where a new stone floor has been laid around the few remaining slabs of the original structure.*

the stone floors, windows and doors of the structure, indiscriminately looted over the decades for use on other properties. It took two years just to dig through the rubble and remove the tenacious ivy which had invaded the interior, a voyage of discovery which revealed intimate details about the keep's original structure. Further reference to books and old archives from neighbouring Birr Castle has enabled Sean to reconstruct the floors and staircases of the keep, fit Gothic windows and even build a massive baronial fireplace in the entrance hall, reputed to have been one of the grandest in Ireland.

A library in the surviving Georgian wing is well underway, and plans for a huge kitchen with storage rooms in the vaulted basement have also been drawn up. As yet there are neither bedrooms nor bathrooms and until the castle is properly habitable the Ryans have chosen to live in the small, cosy gatehouse.

No medieval castle can be without at least one ghost. Indeed, as Sean started to rebuild the keep he was conscious of being observed through unseen eyes and sometimes felt another presence in the room. Two little girls in period dress, thought to be from the Darby family who once lived in the castle, are The Leap's most permanent other-worldly visitors and have been seen on several occasions – the elder of the two sisters, Emily, is known to have fallen from the battlements in the early seventeenth century.

With the Ryans as the custodians of Leap Castle's future, it has become a favourite location for organised tours of reputedly haunted houses in Ireland. Banquets and evenings of music are laid on in the keep during the summer for visiting Americans, at which suckling pig and game are roasted over the hall fire, and ghostly spirits mingle with those of the living as stories unfold down the long refectory table.

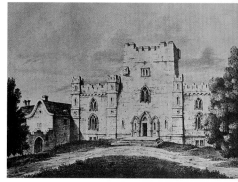

TOP *In the gathering gloom of a winter's afternoon, ravens settle into the trees which have grown up through the remains of one of the castle's Georgian wings.*
ABOVE & OPPOSITE *Leap Castle as it is today, and as it was in its heyday, in an engraving entitled 'The Leap, Seat of Admiral Sir Henry DE Darby KCB'.*

RIGHT *An Indonesian figure fills an alcove in the whitewashed wall of the main entrance hall.* OPPOSITE *Upstairs, on the first floor of the central keep, the main reception room is filled by a large refectory table where banquets are held. A daybed at one end of the room, scattered with colourful Indonesian cushions, has been fashioned from wooden panelling that was salvaged from the stables at nearby Birr Castle.*

ABOVE *The contemporary fresco of a falconer is by Alec Finn, a musician and friend of Sean Ryan. Both belong to an ancient Irish hawking club, and when not playing or restoring, they disappear together over the hills.* OPPOSITE *One corner of the entrance hall has been made more intimate by hanging textiles on the wall and across the draughty doorway. A candelabra casts a warm glow around the room.*

POTTER'S RETREAT

A CASUAL VISITOR TO SHANAGARRY MAY BE FORGIVEN FOR DISCOUNTING IT AS A SMALL, ANONYMOUS VILLAGE SITUATED ON A FLAT AND RELATIVELY UNINTERESTING STRETCH OF THE SOUTH COAST OF IRELAND, JUST EAST OF CORK. Yet its name elicits a curious resonance in both bird lovers and collectors of pottery around the world. The Shanagarry Wetlands, overlooking Ballycotton Bay, are one of the most important staging posts in Europe for migratory birds, and the unassuming village is home to new-wave potter Stephen Pearce, whose workshops and factory produce popular lines of earthenware made from clay dug from the Blackwater River.

A man of enormous energy and drive, Stephen Pearce designed and built his house in 1972 for the princely sum of £6,100, a short distance from the pottery which he set up on his own, following a period working with his father, also a potter. At a time when the accepted building technique in this part of Ireland was to set bungalows on stilts, Stephen opted for a more traditional method and dug a large hole in the ground against the hill, in which his house would be sheltered from the wind.

The ground plan of the house which Stephen designed is identical to that of a traditional Irish cottage, with one central room in which pigs and chickens would have gathered, and a fireplace where the cooking happened. Stephen has successfully revisited the old Irish farmhouse design, drawing on traditional ideas while incorporating several twentieth-century luxuries, such as large windows and underfloor heating.

The Pearce home has come together in stages, each addition to the original plan the result of fundamental changes in Stephen's life. The initial design is based on a simple formula – a symphony of terra-cotta tiles, natural wood and whitewashed walls.

ABOVE *A number of art works around the house are by Patrick Scott, Stephen's godfather and mentor, and are composed using gold leaf and a tempera wash.* OPPOSITE *A modern console table by David Chipperfield which used to display shirts in the Issey Miyake shop in Sloane Street, London, now graces one wall of the conservatory dining room. A selection of hand-made wooden bowls are the work of Ciaran Forbes, a master wood turner and monk at Glenstall Abbey.*

Clutter is banished, each room equipped with deep-set drawers, hidden cupboards and sliding partitions behind which to disguise the detritus produced by his family.

The first major structural change was what he dubbed the 'breeding block', built in 1979 at the far end of the plot, and wholly disconnected from the main house. Here Stephen envisaged raising his children, isolating their noise and clutter from his own space, not realising how impractical this particular vision was to prove. Marriage to his second wife Kim-Mai Mooney and two more children prompted a rethink, and the block was joined to the house by a series of corridors. Family life now gravitates around the central kitchen, aggrandised in 1993 by a light and airy conservatory, which serves as a spacious dining room. The most recent addition to the property has been dubbed the 'Vietnamese Embassy' and is the wing in which his wife's mother now lives.

A scholarship to Japan in 1965 to study pottery rounded off Stephen's education yet he returned to Ireland determined not to copy slavishly what he had seen. Decades later, he is ready to admit that the Japanese way of life has subconsciously influenced nearly everything he has achieved; it is reflected in the harmony and design of his home and his current lifestyle as well as in the design of his pottery.

An acknowledgment of this lasting influence is the tea-house, tucked away on the water's edge at the end of the gardens. What was initially designed as a small hut where Stephen could take a break from his work to eat a sandwich and drink a cup of tea has become a building of stature, influenced by a temple in Japan where Emperors would go and sit to watch the moon rise over the lake. Stephen and Kim-Mai go there to meditate, to watch the birds fly in over the water, and to reflect on life.

ABOVE *A painting by Mick Mulcahy hangs on one wall of the kitchen above a rustic dresser on which a freshly baked loaf of soda bread is cooling.*
OPPOSITE *The small, cosy kitchen links the sitting room and conservatory dining room. Its shelves are filled with Stephen's plates.*

RIGHT & BELOW *The stark, white-washed corridor set wth niches and shelves provides a backdrop for displaying shells gathered at the beach and pottery figures.* OPPOSITE *A stainless steel chair by Philippe Starck is placed like a piece of sculpture in the entrance hall beneath a painting by Felim Egan. The terra-cotta tiles conceal underfloor heating and it is a household custom for shoes to be removed at the front door.*

ABOVE *Stephen designed the circular fire in the tea house, where he and his wife Kim-Mai meditate. The gold-leaf painting is by Patrick Scott.*
LEFT *A view through the massive sliding glass doors of the Japanese-inspired tea house takes in the Shanagarry Wetlands, which are used as a staging post by a multitude of different migratory birds.*

RIGHT *A wall of sliding doors conceals wardrobe space. They are made from canvas on ash-wood frames and are based on Japanese rice paper screens.* OPPOSITE *Stephen has always loved carpentry and the main bedroom is entirely his design. The blueprint for the bed was adapted from a traditional Scandinavian sleigh bed. The bed is made from American ash. The floorboards are Canadian pine.*

GALWAY HAVEN

SPIDDAL IS A SMALL VILLAGE WHICH STRADDLES THE COAST ROAD ALONG THE NORTHERN SHORE OF GALWAY BAY. The houses lining the road appear to be relatively modern, a solitary whitewashed, thatched cottage set apart from its neighbours the only obvious indication of the village's past. At the end of the main street, a rutted road leads down to an old stone pier which shelters a small sandy beach. Beyond the pier, smooth granite boulders are lapped by a gentle swell. The distant mass of the Burren on the opposite shore is just visible across the waters of Galway Bay, calm in the unexpected sunshine of a winter's morning.

Mary McInerney and her partner Mark Norman came to this picturesque spot nine years ago looking for an old house they could do up. They were lucky to acquire a tiny cottage, one of the very few pre-Famine thatched cottages left in the village. The house sits back from the coast, its rough-hewn whitewashed walls and classic red window frames, under its new thatch, in stark contrast to the more contemporary houses which have been built around it over the years. There is no garden, and barely an approach to the cottage, the neighbouring properties sharing the same lane, clustered cheek by jowl on a relatively small plot of land. With so much countryside around, the proximity of these buildings is hard to understand without an explanation of the area's history.

Spiddal was once a village of only thirty houses. Life was hard and the whole community would come together to help build any new property. In the early days, the coast road was designated the King's Highway, which effectively ensured that no houses were built anywhere near it until the end of the eighteenth century. As a result, small houses went up on the edge of the bog, grouped closely together for protection. History relates

ABOVE *A traditional red window frame set in the whitewashed exterior wall of the cottage.* OPPOSITE *A view through what was once the original front door into the conservatory extension which links the cottage with the adjoining stable building.*

that farm animals were used to select the site, since they would always
seek out the driest spot in the field to lie down on. Buildings would have
been raised on the ground where the animals slept at night.

Mary's cottage is of just such a traditional structure. The walls
consist of two rows of stone, filled in between with smaller stones to
keep out the vermin, the outer row falling away so that the rainwater
would drain automatically. The roof would have been laid with wood
and then straw, tied on with a special rope called sugon, a product
unique to Ireland, and from which traditional chair seats are still made.

When Mary bought the cottage, it had already been modernised
with a fitted kitchen and carpets. It was wholly inappropriate and completely lacking in any atmosphere so Mary immediately removed all the contemporary
embellishments. The small rooms are now filled with the legacy of Mary's collecting
days, when she bought and sold antiques. She is still a compulsive visitor of markets and
jumble sales. Her eye for a bargain results in regular purchases, and although she does
not sell any more she continues to buy for herself.

Many of Spiddal's older generation have fond memories of the cottage, and tales
of wild card games and nights of drinking there are part of village folklore. Its transition
from a holiday home to an integral part of the community has been watched and
commented upon with interest. Mary has something of a reputation as a cook, and the
cottage has once again become a place for friends to get together around the long dining
table in the adjoining conservatory to play music, drink and enjoy themselves.

TOP *Smooth granite boulders are revealed on an ebb tide on the shores of Galway Bay.*
ABOVE *Traditional whitewashed cottages cluster along the coast-line. They look out to sea where the three Aran Islands form a natural breakwater across the mouth of Galway Bay.*
OPPOSITE *A neighbour's dog sits in a pool of sunshine against the wall of this traditional thatched cottage, one of only a couple remaining in the village.*

ABOVE *A collection of cups and saucers, jugs, plates and other china bought at markets and sales around the country.* LEFT *A Victorian iron-framed bed almost fills the tiny bright pink guest room. The other bedroom in the cottage is a sleeping platform above the kitchen, while Mary's two daughters have bedrooms in the converted stables.*

ABOVE *The rafters of the low-ceilinged cottage are filled with objects*
Mary has picked up at markets, many of them of a maritime flavour,
since her partner Mark is a marine biologist, and they both enjoy sailing
during the summer. OPPOSITE *The compact kitchen is dominated by a*
large pine dresser crowded with assorted china, and the rafters are hung
with baskets. The folding wooden ladder leads up to a sleeping platform.

RIGHT *The conservatory is a riot of colour, from the deep pink walls and bright cushions on the benches, to the paler pink, red and purple of the winter cactus, geraniums and cut flowers in assorted vases. Marine touches include glass fishing floats and strips of cork. A wicker birdcage suspended from the roof is filled with plastic starfish.* BELOW *A piece of coral and local seashells have been fashioned into a table ornament.*

HIDDEN WORLDS

THE BURREN IS PROBABLY THE MOST EXTRAORDINARY LANDSCAPE IN THE WHOLE OF IRELAND. Situated in north Clare, it covers a vast, bare, hilly area devoid of trees and obvious surface water, a barren stretch of mysterious beauty littered with stones, and dissected by indeterminate lines of dry stone walls. Beneath its limestone surface is a labyrinth of caves, streams and underground lakes. Punctuating the skyline at intervals are strange and beautiful monolithic and megalithic tombs, vast flat stones arranged as monuments to an earlier mystic time. Otherwise the plateau seems uncannily empty and silent, as if no contemporary mortal dares set foot amidst the dolmens and forts of its ancient past.

Yet the Burren's deep sense of mysticism holds a strong attraction for those seeking a more meaningful existence in a world where the pace of life is fast and furious. Within the folds of its terraced mountains and sunken valleys, an amazing variety of houses, cottages and dwellings are tucked away, hidden from the view of passers-by.

Keith Payne is an artist and a traveller who discovered the remains of a small ruin on a patch of land high on the Burren one New Year's Day. Over the ensuing months Keith restored the property and transformed it into a cosy parlour with a huge fireplace, adding a contemporary two-storey house with a huge studio where he works, relaxes and entertains, and a spiral staircase which leads up to a gallery and bedroom. His paintings and drawings, which are displayed all over the house, are strongly influenced by the dolmens and monoliths visible beyond his window.

While mystical places often inspire people to take up new and alternative lifestyles, it is often in these same areas that the last of the traditional craftsmen are found.

ABOVE *The back of one of Gabriel Casey's hawthorn rocking chairs, traditionally known for their relaxing, healing powers.* OPPOSITE *The compact kitchen of Keith Payne's hideaway is planned around the Rayburn, with pots and pans hanging from the ceiling within easy reach.*

Gabriel Casey has lived on the Burren all his life and until 1986 was earning his living as a teacher. During a self-imposed sabbatical, he restored a small cottage and worked for a year along the seashore, collecting seaweed and Irish moss.

He is uncertain how he first became involved in making Irish rustic furniture, but remembers the pleasure he experienced cutting his first length of blackthorn to make a chair. From a small, crowded workshop at the back of his cottage, Gabriel gradually taught himself the ancient skills required to make a traditional Irish rocking chair, always considered an important piece of furniture in any Irish house. Today, his rocking chairs and other rustic furniture have established his reputation as far away as America, where his pieces are prized for the simplicity of their design and the rich colour of the wood.

Gabriel cuts the lengths of hawthorn and blackthorn straight from the hedgerows, their tortured forms lending themselves to the natural shape of the rockers. He starts cutting in the dark of November, on a waning moon, and stores the green wood for nearly eighteen months in an old milling parlour until it has dried sufficiently to work on. Each rocking chair is made with the human form in mind, the length of the rockers, the height of the backposts and the depth of the seat of each chair adapted to fit the individual for whom it is destined.

Gabriel uses traditional tools, each chair worked on lovingly, the knots and unique characteristics of each piece of wood enhanced and burnished with a combination of beeswax and turpentine which brings out the timber's natural colour. The final result resembles more a piece of sculpture than a practical item of furniture and his chairs are instantly recognisable in many homes throughout the Burren.

ABOVE *Wind-blasted trees make strange silhouettes against the darkening sky over the Burren.* OPPOSITE *Lines of dry stone walls are a familiar sight across the Burren's austere landscape.*

LEFT & OPPOSITE *A limestone plateau, the Burren is today empty and silent. Yet signs of the human past are visible everywhere, from dolmens to forts, ancient fields and churches.* BELOW LEFT *Keith Payne's house is framed by the standing stones of the Poulnabrone Dolmen.*

LEFT *Keith's living space is divided into his working studio and a sitting area where a comfortable sofa and mismatched armchair crowd a Scandinavian stove. The traditional rocking chair is by Gabriel Casey. The spiral staircase leads up to a bedroom and gallery.* BELOW *The rustic rope seat of a traditional Irish chair, its rough wooden back and legs bearing the distinctive hallmark of furniture maker Gabriel Casey.*

RIGHT *A traditional rocking chair takes shape in Gabriel's workshop: Lengths of green wood are stacked to dry on shelves at the back of the workshop; a raw, twisted piece of hawthorn is selected; rockers are fitted to the chair at the end.* OPPOSITE *The texture and grain of wood are an obsession for artisans like Gabriel Casey.*

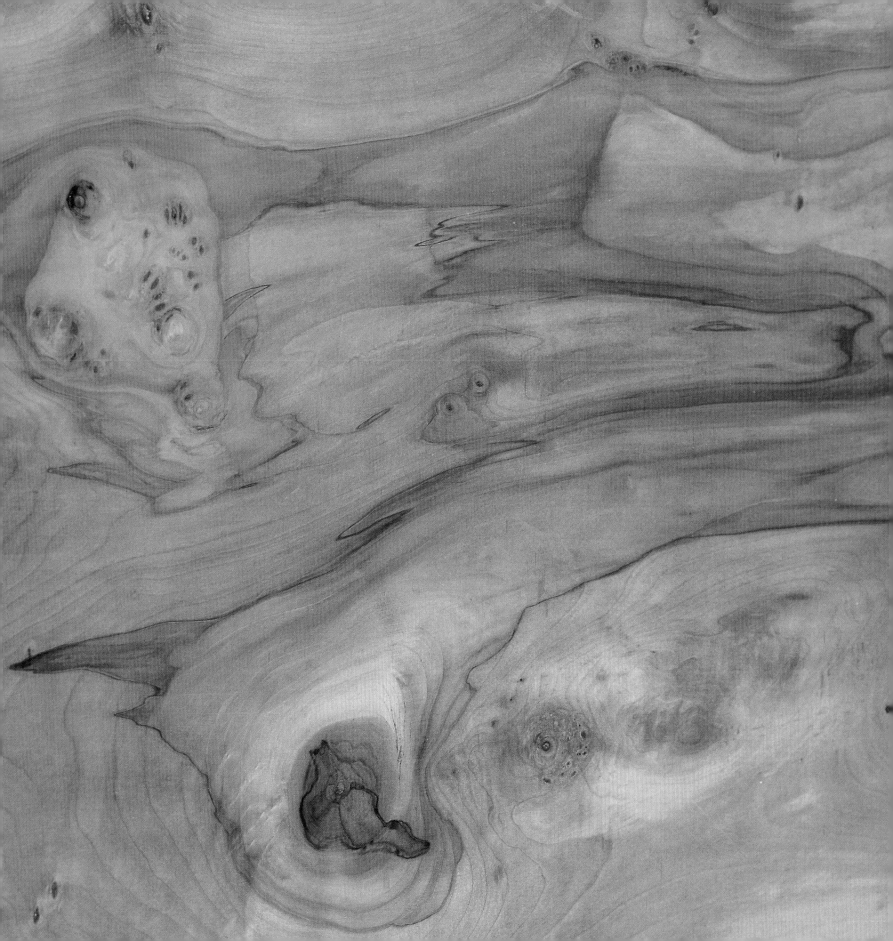

WRITER'S REALM

LOST IN THE BOGS BEYOND SKIBBEREEN IN WEST CORK, THE COTTAGE WHICH AUTHOR VICTORIA GLENDINNING AND HER FAMILY HAVE ENJOYED FOR THE LAST TEN YEARS OR SO STANDS REMOVED FROM THE CURRENT INFLUX OF FOREIGNERS WHO HAVE CHOSEN TO POPULARISE THIS FAR-FLUNG CORNER OF IRELAND, BUYING UP PROPERTY TO RETREAT TO DURING THE SUMMER MONTHS. The approach to Victoria's home is down a winding boreen which leads apparently nowhere. The surrounding marshland is punctuated by the occasional ruined farmhouse and broken gate, and a heron disturbed by the clattering of the cattle-grid rises clumsily out of the reeds. The track is heavy with mud, the water from the bog encroaching relentlessly as the winter storms lash this vulnerable stretch of coast around Roaringwater Bay.

ABOVE *The low ceiling just above the pillow of the guest bed is painted a deep blue on which three turtles are swimming around the names of all those who have slept here – a sort of secret visitor's book.*
OPPOSITE *Ancient walls of upright stones are hidden beneath a cloak of lush green moss. On one the inscription 'Nothing is wasted', a favourite mantra of her late husband, Terence, echoes a second motto in the house, 'Nothing is forever'.*

The cottage stands in a clearing, sheltered by a couple of old stone farm buildings, and beyond it is a small enclosed garden and a lawn, bordered by blue hydrangeas. The marshland gives way to fields at this point and to one side of the cottage an ancient stretch of woodland separates the property from the River Ilen. In spring the woods are a riot of bluebells and primroses, and anemones crowd the riverbank. In winter the river is in spate, the dark water rushing noisily over large granite boulders, submerged for the time being, but from which Victoria and her family swim and sun-bathe in summer. An island in the middle of the river, overgrown and shaded by the overhanging trees, makes an ideal refuge for picnics on warm days.

It is easy to understand how Victoria and her former husband, Terence de Vere White, fell under the spell of this unique spot. They had both lived and worked in Ireland,separately and together, for years. Terence was an Irish author and literary editor

of *The Irish Times*, while Victoria had lived outside Dublin for some time. Her Irish connections were already well established, yet it was not until she was commissioned to write a book about Anthony Trollope, who had worked for the post office in Ireland in the 1840s, that the couple toured Ireland together to visit all the out-of-the-way places in which Trollope had set foot. Originally taken by the rugged, north-east coast of Co. Antrim, it was the harshness of the weather which finally changed their minds in favour of the mild climate and soft green vegetation of Cork, and the beauty of its light.

The main stone cottage is over 500 years old. A more recent addition had been the adjoining conservatory and open-plan room which served as a studio for the artist and his wife who lived there before Victoria bought the property. Improvements to its basic structure were not prompted by any conscious plan, but driven more by the need for a window in a certain place, to stem a leak or to accommodate more people. There was no grand plan, just a few skilled friends, including Bruce who was always on hand to do whatever was needed. Somebody would know of someone 'living on the smell of a rag in the fold of the hills', drawn to the west coast of Ireland, seduced by the landscape and the relaxed pace of life, apparently fleeing their own culture in search of a different life – alternative people who brought their skills with them.

Bruce and his friend are responsible for most things in the house. He came up with a rough plan, and a stream of ideas followed, the application of which was varyingly influenced by time, money and weather. Dealing with old houses is always a gamble – you are never quite sure what you will uncover – but the net result here is a family home of quiet charm, its spirit completely in tune with the natural world which surrounds it.

ABOVE *A bright blue chair leans against the natural stone of a bedroom wall. The door leads to the garden down old slate steps.*
OPPOSITE *A stained-glass door opens from the conservatory on to the kitchen with its beamed ceiling and jolly red oven.*

RIGHT & OPPOSITE *A simple lean-to conservatory links the original 500-year-old cottage with the studio extension. It is furnished comfortably with a few ageing wicker chairs.* BELOW *What once served as a studio for the former owner, artist Terry Searle, is now a dining room, used only if there are too many people to squeeze around the kitchen table.*

ABOVE *The fireplace surround in the sitting room has been plastered and set with shells gathered on beach walks.* RIGHT *The original cottage would have been 'one up, one down' – this cosy red-walled parlour is one of the original rooms of the house and now adjoins the kitchen.*

LEFT *An old bleached wooden chair stands next to a Gothic door which was salvaged by Bruce from a local church. The door has since been painted blue – the colour of west Cork as far as Victoria is concerned.*
OPPOSITE *Dilapidated granite walls zigzag through the surrounding woods which are home to a colony of badgers.*

OVERLEAF *The countryside around Cork has seduced many an outsider into spending the summer months on the west coast of Ireland. For Victoria and her family, the additional magic of the River Ilen and a stretch of woodland at the back of the cottage fulfilled all their dreams.*

A MAP OF IRELAND

PART OF SCOTLAND

ATLANTIC OCEAN

DONEGAL

L. DERRY   ANTRIM

TYRONE   ULSTER   OMAGH   CARRICKFERGUS   BELFAST

FERMANAGH   MONAGHAN   ARMAGH   DOWN

SLIGO   LEITRIM   CAVAN   LOUTH

MAYO   ROSCOM   LONGFORD   E MEATH

CONNAUGHT   MON   W MEATH   TRIM

GALWAY   ATHENRY   KINGS C.   DUBLIN   DUB   HARBOUR

GALWAY BAY   LEINSTER   KILD   WICK LOW

CLARE   ENNIS   QUEENS   MARYBOROUGH   BARO   CAR LOW

LIMERICK   TIPPE   RARY   KILKENNY   WEX FORD

SHANNON   CLONMEL   KEN NY

MUNSTER   WATERFORD   HARBOUR

KERRY   TRALEE   CORK   YOUGHAL BAY

DINGLE BAY   KILLARNEY   MIZEN HEAD

IRISH CHANNEL

HOLY HEAD

SOUTH WALES

IRISH MILES
ENGLISH

85 ENG M.

Wrought by HANNAH LECKY CORK 1809

IRELAND GUIDE

NORTHERN IRELAND

• HOTELS & GUEST HOUSES

The Bushmills Inn

25 Main Street

Bushmills, Co. Antrim

tel: 012657 32339

A seventeenth-century coaching inn

near the Giant's Causeway.

Edenvale House

130 Portaferry Road

Newtownards, Co. Down

tel: 01247 814881

Built in 1780, a bed & breakfast

near Strangford Lough.

The Narrows

8 Shore Road

Portaferry, Co. Down

tel: 012477 28148

The Narrows guest house sits right

by the waters of Strangford Lough.

Simply decorated rooms have

views out over the water, and the

restaurant serves delicious seafood.

Tempo Manor

Tempo

Co. Fermanagh

tel: 013655 41953

A centuries' old family home has

been turned into a romantic lakeside

bed & breakfast with shooting and

fishing facilities.

• RESTAURANTS

Ginger Tree

29 Ballyrobert Road

Ballyclare, Co. Antrim

tel: 01232 848176

A Japanese restaurant in a Victorian

farmhouse. The speciality is grilled

Lough Neagh eel.

Roscoff

7 Lesley House

Shaftesbury Square

Belfast, Co. Antrim

tel: 01232 331532

Chef Paul Rankin opened Roscoff

a decade ago and has maintained

the restaurant's deserved reputation.

Ramore

The Harbour

Portrush, Co. Antrim

tel: 01265 824313

Spectacular views of the harbour and

a menu which is constantly changing.

Shanks

The Blackwood

150 Crawfordsburn Road

Bangor, Co. Down

tel: 01247 853313

The innovative menu makes good use

of local ingredients. Situated in the

Blackwood golf centre with interior

designed by Sir Terence Conran.

• SPECIALITIES

Northern Salmon Company

Glenarm, Co. Antrim

tel: 01574 841 691

Delicious fresh and smoked salmon.

Glenarm Pottery

Glenarm, Co. Antrim

tel: 01574 841 013

For works by local potters.

DUBLIN & ENVIRONS

• HOTELS & GUEST HOUSES

Red House

Ardee, Co. Louth

tel: 041 53523

A Georgian house set in forty acres of

woodland and garden. Serves excellent

Irish breakfasts.

Ghan House

Carlingford

Co. Louth

tel: 042 937 3682

An eighteenth--century house enclosed

by the walls of medieval Carlingford.

Also has a popular restaurant.

Belcamp Hutchinson

Malahide Road

Balgriffin, Dublin 17

tel: 01 846 0843

A country house hotel about

20 minutes from the centre of Dublin.

The Clarence

6-8 Wellington Quay

Dublin 2

tel: 01 670 9000

Owned by U2 frontman, Bono,

The Clarence is the hip place to stay,

with stylish decor and a distinguished

restaurant, The Tea Room.

Number 31

31 Leeson Close

Dublin 2

tel: 01 676 5011

An old coach house and adjoining

Georgian house in a mews, this is a

discreet hotel in the heart of Dublin.

Butlers Town House

44 Landsdowne Road

Ballsbridge, Dublin 4

tel: 01 667 4022

A converted Victorian town house

serving delicious Irish breakfasts in

tasteful surroundings.

• RESTAURANTS

Commons

85-86 St. Stephen's Green

Dublin 2

tel: 01 478 0530

Modern brasserie with rococo interiors.

L'Ecrivain

109a Lower Baggot Street

Dublin 2

tel: 01 661 1919

The yellow dining room is hung with

portraits of Irish writers, from James

Joyce to Seamus Heaney.

Peacock Alley

Fitzwilliam Hotel

119 St. Stephen's Green

Dublin 2

tel: 01 677 0708

Contemporary Irish cooking set

within the chic Fitzwilliam Hotel.

Patrick Guilbaud

21 Upper Merrion Street

Dublin 2

tel: 01 676 4192

Located in the Merrion Hotel, with

its own gardens, this restaurant serves

classic, yet modern, food.

Les Fréres Jacques

74 Dame Street

Dublin 2

tel: 01 679 4555

Chef Nicolas Boutin serves a wide

variety of fresh fish from this bustling

French restaurant situated next door

to the Olympia Theatre.

• SPECIALITIES

Hodges Figgis

56-58 Dawson Street

Dublin 2

tel: 01 677 4754

For a good selection of books,

in particular Irish literature.

DESIGNyard

12 East Essex Street

Temple Bar, Dublin 2

tel: 01 677 8453

For traditional and modern Irish crafts.

The Dalkey Design Company

20 Railway Road

Dalkey, Co. Dublin

tel: 012 856 827

Design store owned by Glynis Robins

(whose home is featured on pages 66-73).

The Ha' Penny Bridge Galleries

15 Bachelors Walk

Dublin 1

tel: 01 453 4593

For art and antiques.

Lantern Antiques

56 Francis Street

Dublin 8

tel: 01 453 4593

For Irish antiques.

Brown Thomas Linen Shop

88-95 Grafton Street

Dublin 2

tel: 01 679 5666

For traditional fine Irish linens,

including table and bed linen.

THE SOUTH & WEST

• HOTELS & GUEST HOUSES

Tullanisk

Birr

Co. Offaly

tel: 0509 20572

The Georgian dower house to Birr Castle

(as featured on pages 54–63).

The Castle

Castletownshend

Nr. Skibbereen, Co. Cork

tel: 028 36100

An atmospheric sixteenth-century

castle right by the sea.

Spinner's Town House

Birr, Co. Offaly

tel: 0509 21673

Five Georgian houses comprising a

guest house with bistro and art gallery.

Liss Ard Lake Lodge

Skibbereen

Co. Cork

tel: 028 40000

An unusual hotel (featured on pages 116-27) with organic restaurant, situated beside Lough Abisdealy.

Ballylickey Manor

Bantry Bay

Co. Cork

tel: 027 50071

This 300-year-old shooting lodge is owned by the nephew of the poet Robert Graves.

Bantry House

Bantry

Co. Cork

tel: 027 50047

A wonderful country house overlooking Bantry Bay, it has been in the same family since 1739.

Gregans Castle

Ballyvaughan

Co. Clare

tel: 065 707 7005

Dating from the seventeenth century, Gregans Castle is near the wild landscape of The Burren.

Temple House

Ballymote

Co. Sligo

tel: 071 83329

Everything about this property is huge including the massive bedrooms.

• RESTAURANTS

Ballymaloe House

Shanagarry

Co. Cork

tel: 021 652531

Home of Myrtle Allen's famous restaurant and cooking school.

Rosleague Manor

Letterfrack

Co. Galway

tel: 095 41101

First-class restaurant in a hotel over-looking the wild coast of Connemara.

• SPECIALITIES

Stephen Pearce Pottery

Shanagarry

Co. Cork

tel: 021 646 807

Pottery by Stephen Pearce (as featured on pages 166-75) can be purchased directly from the gallery in Shanagarry.

Gabriel Casey

The Burren

Co. Clare

tel: 065 707 4765

Famous for his rustic Irish furniture (as featured on pages 186-95).

Index

Note: references in *italics* are to captions.

Acknowledgments

The publishers extend sincere thanks to all those who graciously allowed their homes to be photographed, and regret that not all could be included in the end. Thanks also to Marianne Faithfull, Rosemary Hamilton, Dorothy Mitchell-Smith and Elizabeth Gain.

The author would like to thank Victoria Lloyd and Hector McDonnell for all their help as well as Pom Lampson for running the office so beautifully.

Marianne Faithfull thanks her friends in Ireland for their support – you know who you are.

Photographs: pages 3 & 5, photographed on the Leixlip Estate, with thanks to the Guinness family.